What Others Are Saying About *Simple Spirituality*

"This is a challenging and appealing book. It reveals the part of love to Jesus and of Jesus—presence to the poor, the broken and the vulnerable. Chris has a gentle and realistic way of showing that this path which can appear as austere, suffering and insecure is tempered, rendered human and Christian and even enjoyable through meetings of love and of tenderness, which heal us, liberate us, give us strength and new life."

—**Jean Vanier,** founder of the communities of L'Arche and author of *Becoming Human*

"For those of us in the affluent West, spirituality has become muddled by materialism and complicated by our frenetic pace of life. Chris Heuertz helps to unwind the suffocating insulation that cocoons us and stunts our spiritual growth. From his amazing array of experiences among the poor, Chris has been educated in the seminary of the slums. In this deep but accessible work, he draws us alongside the prostitutes, the dying, the disabled and the beggars to help us learn what he has learned—that sitting so close to the heart of God, the poor have the proximity and perspective to teach us the art of simple spirituality."

—**Scott A. Bessenecker, director,** InterVarsity Global Projects, and author of *The New Friars*

"There's no doubt about it: Chris Heuertz has found Jesus among the poorest of the poor—a Jesus who calls us to humility, community, simplicity, submission and brokenness. Throughout *Simple Spirituality,* as he shares his experiences from around the globe, he challenges and inspires us all to seek Jesus and follow him with renewed passion and integrity. Read it and be transformed."

—**Stephen A. Seamands,** professor of Christian doctrine, Asbury Theological Seminary

11/11

"Chris Heuertz's ability to weave real-life stories with scriptural and theological reflection makes this a very engaging and refreshing book. At a time when the gap between the poor and rich continues to grow, Chris reminds us that what the gospel commands us to do is not so much to do things for the poor but to become friends, indeed sit at the same table, with the poor. What makes such a duty possible, even delightful, are such gifts as humility, community, simplicity, submission and brokenness—simple spirituality, he calls it!"

—**Emmanuel Katongole**, associate research professor of theology and world Christianity, and codirector of the Center for Reconciliation, Duke Divinity School

"Chris Heuertz's *Simple Spirituality: Learning to See God in a Broken World* brings three critical transforming themes together—simplicity, spirituality and our broken world— through very simple, real-life narratives. The book not only meets a critical need in the mission world but raises critical questions for those working among the poor and the oppressed. Chris and his wife, Phileena, have been a blessing—people of passion and simplicity. I am sure readers will be blessed."

—**Jayakumar Christian**, national director, World Vision India

"Chris Heuertz has written a thoughtful, compelling invitation to think, trust and act more deeply in faith. He is aware of the enormous challenges we face and of the thickness of anxiety that can undermine faith. In the midst of that, he keeps his head clear, his heart focused and his words accessible. This book will be a source of strength and encouragement among those who are serious about 'following.'"

—**Walter Brueggemann**, Professor Emeritus, Columbia Theological Seminary

"Through his personal vulnerability, tender insights and unflinching truthfulness, Chris Heuertz invites readers to see, love and live more fully. *Simple Spirituality* is a compelling book with an important message."

—**Christine D. Pohl**, professor of social ethics, Asbury Theological Seminary

CHRISTOPHER L. HEUERTZ

SIMPLE
SPIRITUALITY

LEARNING TO SEE GOD
IN A BROKEN WORLD

Foreword by SHANE CLAIBORNE

IVP Books
An imprint of InterVarsity Press
Downers Grove, Illinois

InterVarsity Press
P.O. Box 1400, Downers Grove, IL 60515-1426
World Wide Web: www.ivpress.com
E-mail: email@ivpress.com

InterVarsity Press® is the book-publishing division of InterVarsity Christian Fellowship/USA®, a movement of students and faculty active on campus at hundreds of universities, colleges and schools of nursing in the United States of America, and a member movement of the International Fellowship of Evangelical Students. For information about local and regional activities, write Public Relations Dept., InterVarsity Christian Fellowship/USA, 6400 Schroeder Rd., P.O. Box 7895, Madison, WI 53707-7895, or visit the IVCF website at <www.intervarsity.org>.

Many names throughout the book have been changed to protect the identity of the people.

All Scripture quotations, unless otherwise indicated, are taken from the Holy Bible, Today's New International Version™ Copyright © 2001 by International Bible Society. All rights reserved.

Design: Matt Smith
Images: Veer

ISBN 978-0-8308-3621-5

Printed in the United States of America ∞

Library of Congress Cataloging-in-Publication Data

Heuertz, Christopher L., 1971-
 Simple spirituality: learning to see God in a broken world /
Christopher L. Heuertz.
    p. cm.
 Includes bibliographical references.
 ISBN 978-0-8308-3621-5 (pbk.: alk. paper)
 1. Spirituality 2. Christian life. I. Title.
 BV4501.3.H49 2008
 248.4—dc22

                                                               2008008909

P   24   23   22   21   20   19   18   17   16   15   14   13   12   11   10   9   8   7   6   5   4   3
Y   28   27   26   25   24   23   22   21   20   19   18   17   16   15   14   13   12   11   10   09

For Phileena.

Thanks for believing in my voice.

Your life and love have been

my inspiration.

CONTENTS

FOREWORD

It's a fun time to be alive. So much is stirring up in the church and in the world. A new evangelicalism has emerged in post–religious-right America, and we are seeing a Christianity that is closer to the poor, further from the drums of war, a Christianity that looks a little more like Jesus.

Chris Heuertz is one of the most important voices in the movement to reimagine global missions in the twenty-first century. For Heuertz and the Word Made Flesh family, the missionary life is not compartmentalized or fragmented, and missions is certainly not just a trip you do for two weeks every summer. Missions is a way of life. Every Christian is called to live missionally, to seek first the kingdom of God over the empires of this world—no longer as venturesome Westerners who go to an island of "barbarians" to translate the Bible for them. We are to live as missionaries whether we are doctors, students, scientists, teachers or jobless.

Though he was on a mission, Jesus was not simply a "missionary" to the poor. He *was* poor. He joined the suffering of humanity and entered into the human struggle from the day he was born in the manger till the moment he was executed on the cross. In Jesus we see God entering this world as a baby refugee in the middle of a genocide, wandering the streets with "no place to lay his head" and dying next to two bandits on the imperial cross. It is this Jesus who we are invited to follow.

Like the world in which Jesus was born, ours is one of big beasts and little prophets. There are many giants that stand in the way of God's dream. But the great irony is that we have a God that uses the foolish things to confound the wise, the weak things to shame the strong. The great paradox and humor of God's audacious power is this: a stuttering prophet will be the voice of God, a barren old lady will become the mother of a nation, a shepherd boy will become their king, and a homeless baby will lead them home.

Even in the most tumultuous and confusing eras, when Christianity is in danger of being infected by the culture of crusades and markets, there are always the little voices crying out in the wilderness, "Another world is possible!" Chris Heuertz is one of those little prophets. He's ready to take on the beasts, the Goliaths of this age. But, like David, he doesn't need the armor or artillery of war—he just needs a few smooth stones and a little kid's slingshot.

For Heuertz, the stones to slay the giants of our age are the "lifestyle celebrations" of the Word Made Flesh family—humility, community, simplicity, submission, brokenness. They are not the weapons of power but the peculiar weapons of the upside-down kingdom of God. I love that Chris calls these pillars of discipleship "celebrations." We social justice types can be so serious and obsessed with what we are against that we forget to celebrate the things we are for. After all, it's much easier to protest than it is to protestify—and this is not just a book about what's wrong, but it points us to the things that can correct the messes that we have made of this world. Chris reminds us what we are for: In a world of arrogance we are for humility. In a world of individualism we are for community. In a world of excess we are for simplicity. In a world of power we are for submission. In a world of triumphalism we are for brokenness.

Much of Christianity has been so driven by evangelism that we have created a church that has become filled with "believers" but where disciples are rather hard to come by. Years ago, I found myself in that place where I knew I was a "believer" but I had no idea what it meant to be a follower of Jesus. It is easy to worship Jesus without following him. Pop Christianity radio and TV preachers talk about how God wants to bless you, how if you give a dollar you will get a hundred back. (Do you ever wonder why they are so desperate for money? Haha.) Lining the shelves are books on finding the secret to success, discovering your purpose, finding your best life. But if we are not careful, we miss the truth at the heart of Jesus: if we want to find our life, we should give it away for others. We are made to live for something bigger than ourselves. The best thing to do with the best things in life is to give them away.

This is not a snub book about guilt or even about how the poor need you. This is a book about a spirituality that leads us all to life— about how the poor need the rich and the rich need the poor, and how all of us are in need of God. This is the gospel that comforts the disturbed and disturbs the comfortable—but it is a gospel that is good news to all of us. This is the message of Chris Heuertz.

Amid all the promising campaigns to "Make Poverty History," Chris Heuertz reminds us that it is equally important to make poverty personal. Mother Teresa, who has been a great teacher of his and mine, used to say: "It is very fashionable to talk about the poor. Unfortunately it is not as fashionable to talk to the poor." If we truly care about the poor, we can name them. They are our friends—people from whom we learn, with whom we cry and laugh and jump in fire hydrants. In this book, Chris tells us stories from the ground, from the slums and ghettoes, from people who have truly made the issues of poverty personal. There is a beautiful Scripture where Jesus tells the disciples, "I no longer call you servants, but I call you friends." This book is an invitation to reject the world's dream of autonomy and comfort, to follow Jesus to the margins of the empire in which we live and to become friends of the poor.

Heuertz calls us to follow Jesus, to find Christ in his most distressing disguises in the forsaken corners of our world. Some of you will go to the slums after reading this book. I hope you do (and if you do, go with Word Made Flesh!). But not everyone will go to the slums. And that is the beauty of Chris's vision. He knows the truth that we learned from Mother Teresa: "Calcuttas are everywhere. Lepers are all around us if we will only have the eyes to see." This is not just a book for people who are ready to go to the slums. It is a book for people who are ready to see that the slums are all around us, people who want to have new eyes to see the poor right in front of us.

Shane Claiborne

INTRODUCTION

On Sight, Spirituality and Stones

As soon as Safi entered the room, I knew there was something amazing about him. Although he can't see, he perceives more than most people ever will. He grew up in an orphanage in Kolkata (formerly Calcutta), India. I met him around Christmas when he was eleven years old. A family in the United States had just adopted him, and he was soon leaving for his new home. That night he was saying goodbye to some dear friends.

The first time he heard me speak, he immediately asked in his high, spunky voice, "Who's that?" As if he could see exactly where I stood, he boldly crossed the room and walked right up to me.

Safi made me feel like family. So warm, so friendly, so kind. I was amazed throughout the evening as I watched him interact with the group. He knew everyone in the room, and when someone spoke to him, Safi would walk right over to where the voice was coming from and start up the liveliest conversation.

That night we came together as a community to share a meal. After dinner someone took out a guitar and started playing. Safi loves music and made a beeline to the guitar. He leaned his head against the base of the guitar and started strumming along as my friend played the chords. It was astonishing to watch this little guy play the instrument like a pro. We all sat in awe of his performance.

Later that evening, we dimmed the lights, a few candles were lit, and the fourteen people present gathered in a circle to pray. The room was still until Safi suddenly chirped, "Where's Chris?" Quietly, I answered, "Over here." With poise he walked right up to me.

Safi held everyone's attention as he spoke to us of prayer. His thoughts on prayer were profound, and his confidence that God would answer them humbled me. I believed Safi's faith could move mountains.

I asked Safi, "What should we pray for? What do you want?"

He didn't even pause to think. "I want to see."

In the dim candlelight, every one of us tried to hold back the tears as this child's faith convicted us. He turned to me and asked, "What do you want?" My heart sank inside me. What could I say? My voice cracked as I softly and slowly replied, "I also want you to see." Tears rolled down my cheeks.

With that, Safi led us in prayer. "Jesus, give me the eyes!"

BEGGING FOR SIGHT

Mine is the story of a blind man receiving sight. I have the physical eyes that Safi longs for, but I often don't know how to use them.

My story begins when I was a university student. I had decided to spend the summer between my junior and senior year traveling through Asia, volunteering for organizations that worked among the poor. After making stops in Korea, Malaysia, Singapore, Thailand, Nepal and Bangladesh, I arrived in South India and eventually made my way north to Kolkata, finding my way to the convent where Mother Teresa was living.

I stood outside and apprehensively knocked on the door. A young nun greeted me and welcomed me inside. I explained my desire to volunteer for the next seven weeks, and she graciously put me to work. I was sent to *Nirmal Hriday*, "The Place of the Pure Heart."

Nirmal Hriday, commonly known as "The House for the Dying," was the first home opened by Mother Teresa and the Missionaries of Charity. It's a sort of communal hospice, bustling with activity as nuns and volunteers serve side by side to bathe, feed and comfort their guests. Since 1952, *Nirmal Hriday* has welcomed nearly 100,000 men and women, offering them dignity and love as they pass from this life into the next.

A simple building, the House for the Dying shares a wall with the Kali temple, dedicated to the Hindu goddess of death. In this strange corner, death is both worshiped and mourned. In one sacred space, goats are sacrificed on a daily basis (not to mention the rumor that infants are still offered as human sacrifices to Kali). In the other sacred space, death is grieved and poverty considered an insult against the imprint of God's image in humanity.[1]

The home is surrounded by the hustle and bustle of Kolkata's crowded streets—streets filled with people begging, looking for spare change and digging through the trash. As I entered the home for the first time, I could never have prepared myself for how my life was about to change.

Before I reached the top of the three small stairs leading to the door of *Nirmal Hriday*, my ears were flooded with soft cries, moans and coughs—a literal cacophony of misery—from those dying just beyond the door. I was immediately overwhelmed before even stepping foot into the home. Once past the threshold, my eyes adjusted from the intense Indian sun to the dimly lit room. The initial images that met me were the most heartbreaking I had ever seen.

The home consists of two wards, one side for the men and the other side for the women, each with fifty beds. Before me were men of all ages, dying bodies barely covering their souls. By their appearance many actually seemed healthy, but many more were emaciated, dehydrated, wasting away and starved. The grievous sight was accompanied by a nameless odor, maybe the smell of death. In this place, the living resembled the dead, many looking like corpses awaiting burial.

The imminence of death, however, was muted by the celebration of life. Many of the men sitting in their beds raised their hands, palms together in the typical gesture of respect to welcome me. The tender touch and love radiated by the nuns reminded me that God is often nearest to those who seem the furthest from God.

I was just a student. Up to this point I had lived a fairly protected and sheltered life. I could not believe my eyes. I could not imagine any other place on earth where one would find such graphic and explicit human suffering complemented with a presence of God's peace and tranquility. The home had a contemplative tone about it, as though the presence of Christ himself filled the space. The golden sunlight pouring through the windows, the quiet, the prayerful way the nuns and volunteers cared for those dying all contributed to a real sense of hope.

I introduced myself to the head of the volunteers, an animated German man named Andy. After a few conciliatory words of welcome, he pointed to four dead bodies stacked beside the door— mere skeletons wrapped in pure white sheets, except one that was drenched through with blood and had attracted a swarm of flies. Time seemed to stop. I stood there blinking—trying to comprehend what I was looking at. Abruptly Andy told me to help carry the bodies outside and place them in an ambulance.

As I carried the stiff and weightless corpses, the blood left a red trail and a stench that was nearly unbearable. The bodies were loaded onto the vehicle and taken to a Hindu temple where they were to be cremated.

During those first seven weeks at the House for the Dying, I attended to nearly fifty dead bodies. Although I have been back many times since my first visit in 1993, I have never become accustomed to the suffering. I have never gotten used to death, no matter how predictable and inevitable it may seem.

One day I came in early to help wash the dishes from afternoon tea. I was the only volunteer present as two men brought an older man to the home on a stretcher. They had found him at the train station in awful shape. He was a Muslim, maybe in his sixties, and very sick.

I brought him to the washroom at the back of the home and began giving him a bath. He was so malnourished and weak that he could not sit up properly, so I leaned him against the corner of the bathroom and began washing his hair. It was matted and full of lice. I had to shave his head and his long beard. As I washed his face, I noticed he was blind. His eye sockets were full of thick mucus, and every time I tried to wash them he cried out in agony.

After washing his body, I tried to wash his feet, but one of them was mutilated and covered with decaying skin. It is likely that while the man was lying on the train platform, a dog or some rats nibbled away at his toes, leaving the insides of his flesh exposed. What was left of his foot was full of maggots, eating away at the infection that was festering within his open wound. I did what I could to clean his foot, but picking at the worms with a pair of tweezers was ineffective; it would take several days to get rid of them all.

After his bath I dressed him, carried him to a bed and prepared a bit of lunch so that he could eat. He was so weak that he could not take the food orally, so with the help of the head nun, Sister Luke, we prepared something else and fed him nasally. The nasal-fed patients were generally the weakest in the home and, once admitted, seemed to live only a few days.

After only a week of care, the blind man surprisingly regained enough strength to start eating again. Of course, for a while we still had to help feed him. I spent hours each day with this man. Holding his hands, singing to him, praying for him, trying to talk to him even though I am sure he did not speak English, I hoped that in some miraculous way God was ministering love to him simply through my presence.

Another week passed and he slowly began feeding himself. His foot was also showing signs of healing, and the mucus that had filled his eye sockets had dried up. Sister Luke decided he was healthy enough to be discharged. He would go to a leprosarium, where what was left of his foot would be amputated and he would receive further treatment.

As I carried him to the taxi that would take him away, he clenched my hand, and tears covered both our faces. I never saw that man again.

Later that night, back in the room I was renting from a widow in the city, I opened the Scriptures to Luke 18:35-43. The Gospel passage tells of a time when Jesus was traveling on the road from Jerusalem to Jericho. A crowd had gathered and was following Jesus. A blind man, begging at the side of the road, heard the commotion and asked what was happening. "Jesus of Nazareth is passing by," they replied.

Perhaps having heard the stories of this great healer, the blind man mustered up the courage to cry out to him: "Jesus, Son of David, have mercy on me!"

Much like today, the people tried to silence the one who was begging. They scolded and hassled the blind man. The crowd didn't want to bother Jesus with the ranting and raving of one whom society discarded. However, of all the people in the crowd that day, the Gospels indicate that Jesus stopped only for him, asking simply, "What do you want me to do for you?"

It's an awkward situation. Surely it was obvious to Jesus, as well as to the crowd, that the man was blind. But Jesus wanted him to recognize his need. The man said simply, "Lord, I want to see." Luke tells us that Jesus healed him immediately.

I sat on my bed that summer night in Kolkata and made the connections. The blind man begging in the story reminded me of the blind Muslim man I had been caring for over the past few weeks. As

I prayed for understanding, it was as if God was opening my own blind eyes. Suddenly another connection was made—*my* blindness to his. I too was blind.

For all the time I had spent with the Muslim man in the House for the Dying, I had missed seeing what God had been trying to show me: my inability and unwillingness to see God's hand outstretched and awaiting my grasp. The Scriptures filled in the gaps and showed me that *I* was the one begging. My pride, selfishness, lusts, fears, insecurities, my need for significance and acceptance were all begging from those who could never satisfy my hungers. The woundedness in me had blinded my own self-perception.

In my blindness, unable to see my God-given dignity and identity, I perceived myself through false identities. True to my evangelical upbringing, I saw myself as sinful and selfish. I saw myself through my own woundedness and insecurities. I saw myself as mean, uncompassionate, cold-hearted and unresponsive. I was hard on myself; I wouldn't forgive myself and instead, I let shame rule in my heart.

In my inability to see God's nearness I had tried to create a self-sufficient way of living. In the dark, I was trying to find my way to God rather than allowing myself to be discovered by God's love. I became god unto myself, playing the divine role of Creator (by trying to make myself a better person), Judge (by telling myself how bad I was, how unworthy I had become before God) and Redeemer (by trying to earn grace, to be *good enough* for it). I realized that I desperately needed God's eyes to help me see the way to God's heart.

BLINDNESS OR BLIND PEOPLE?

I find it a painfully vulnerable task to introduce my blindness in this book. I am a part of a community called Word Made Flesh, a group of people called and committed to serving Jesus among the most vulnerable of the world's poor. We are covenanted together by a shared spirituality with missional implications. This process and path of discovery takes us all around the world to slums and sewers, refugee camps and red-light districts. We literally live among the dying as an act of solidarity with our neighbors and our God. We don't assume to have answers, but together in community with and among our friends who are poor[2] we seek to discover Jesus. And yet I realize, much like the blind man whom Jesus healed at the pool of Bethsaida (Mark 8:22-25), that having my eyes opened doesn't mean I am immediately able to understand what I'm seeing. I also must confess that even though Jesus has given me sight, I still like to squint, and sometimes I even prefer not to look.[3]

A while back I was inspired by the great holiness preacher Dennis Kinlaw to read at least one book by every author who had ever been awarded the Nobel Prize for Literature.[4] That's a long list. Either I chose the wrong books or I just don't have a properly developed appreciation for good literature: out of every four or five books I read from that list, I wished I'd only read one.

One of the few memorable reads was the novel *Blindness* by the Portuguese author José Saramago. The story starts out in a traffic jam, as an unsuspecting motorist suddenly loses his vision at a stoplight.

It gets worse.

Throughout the city people are going blind for no apparent reason. It's an outbreak. The authorities panic and quarantine all the victims of this unusual plague. Soon the very soldiers imprisoning this blind population start to lose their vision. There's a power struggle, and people who were actually blind before the outbreak realize that they hold an advantage over a newly blinded population. Those born blind have been forced to learn to live with their blindness, while the newly blinded are struggling to make sense of their new reality. Chaos ensues. It gets really nasty. Things get ugly fast.

Ironically, no one is spared from the pandemic except the wife of an ophthalmologist. She fakes blindness in order to protect herself from becoming the overused eyes for everyone. Toward the end of the story, people suddenly, inexplicably but gloriously begin to recover their eyesight, and the ophthalmologist's wife begins to grapple with the crisis of this experience—she never knew what it was like to be blind and is subsequently disconnected from everyone else's collective rediscovery of vision.

As you can imagine, the book is packed full of symbols and metaphors of light, vision, perception and even faith. Saramago writes, "It used to be said there is no such thing as blindness, only blind people, when the experience of time has taught us nothing other than that there are no blind people, only blindness."⁵ Really, I think he's right. I believe we all have access to sight—the vision of self-reflection, the ability to see God's intentions for each of us, and the possibility of looking into a future smothered in the loving embrace of God—if only we can find it, and only if we're able to receive the grace to accept it.

My spiritual director, Father Larry Gillick, is a Jesuit priest and the director of the Delgman Center for Ignatian Spirituality. He lost his sight when he was four years old. In an article he wrote for St. John's Church on the campus of Creighton University, he noted that "people who are blind from birth, or who received this gift early in their lives, do not know what they look like."⁶ And yet, in the truest sense, do any of us *really* know what we look like? Often it seems I am blind to the goodness of God, to God's leading in my life, to the destiny God has for me. I'm reduced to begging for attention, affection and affirmation in the wrong ways and in the wrong places.

The modern mystic and Cistercian monk Thomas Keating suggests that humanity is born with essential biological needs that lay claim on our lives. Pursuing their fulfillment creates unreasonable and unrealistic demands on our souls, and the deep unhappiness that results keeps us from discovering our true selves—it is a kind of blindness: "The human condition [is] to be without the true source of happiness, which is the experience of the presence of God."[7] Resonating with Saramago, Keating would suggest that there are no blind people, only the spiritual blindness of the human condition.

PLAYING DRESS UP

Sometimes perspective is everything. Sometimes our perspective blinds us in such a way that we can't properly hear what we can't see past. Too often we make complicated what really is very simple.

Several years after my first visit to the House for the Dying, in what seemed to be a completely different world, the U.S. Department of State invited me, as a representative of Word Made Flesh, to a conference on combating sex-trafficking.[8] The thing that stood out most to me in the invitation was that dress was to be formal.

I don't like to dress up. In fact, I call my flip-flops "work shoes" and wear shorts to the office more than 85 percent of the year (even in Omaha's subzero winters). I spend a lot of my time around the world with kids who live on the streets, children dying from AIDS, former child soldiers, and women and children forced to prostitute themselves. My friends overseas don't really care what I wear. So I called the State Department, wondering if I could come as I am.

The State Department *did* care what I wore. I was told that I needed to dress formally.

A couple days later I called them back, this time a little embarrassed. I didn't even own a suit. They informed me that the vice president of Colombia, a Supreme Court justice from India, the U.S. secretary of state and even the president of the United States would likely be attending, and thus I needed to dress up.

To me all black suits look the same, so I ran off to Sears to buy the cheapest black suit I could find. At the conference I felt like I blended in perfectly, though I'm sure all the suit-snobs were wondering, *Why in the world is he wearing that?*

A couple of years later I was invited to speak for the missions conference of a midwestern Christian university. I speak at a lot of colleges, so I filled my backpack with my standard gear: my best pair of pants—some distressed jeans from the Gap, a couple of collared shirts, some really cool (at least I think so) T-shirts, and my trusty old flip-flops.

Moments before I was to speak in the first chapel service, a student approached me, visibly troubled. He reluctantly informed me that I was in violation of their campus dress code for chapel speakers. Unfortunately for me, it wasn't just a rule or two that I was breaking; there were numerous violations. While I was able to take out my earrings, my shoes and pants were still unacceptable. I think I would have been fine speaking barefoot, but I sort of wanted to keep my pants on.

Immediately after the service, the dean of the chapel rushed up on the stage. I could tell he was perturbed, so before he could start the confrontation, I apologized, letting him know that I just realized I had broken their rules and explaining that no one had informed me of this standard. I assured him that I meant no harm or insult to his community, that I had brought my best clothes to speak in. Frustrated, he mentioned that this was not the first such instance of miscommunication and that his secretary would be hearing from him. He walked away, almost in mid-conversation, leaving me wondering what to do.

Later that night I got a call from some students in one of the guys' dorms. They were worried about me and were trying to come up with some clothes my size from guys on their hall. I thanked them and let them know that the dean knew I had brought my best clothes and was understanding.

First thing the next morning I found the dean and mentioned the previous evening's call. I told him I didn't want my clothes to take away from the credibility of what I had come to share. I was actually speaking on submission that morning, and I was willing to submit to their community, so I volunteered to drive into town and buy some clothes that would be acceptable for a chapel speaker. The dean brightened up at the suggestion and asked, "Would you like to do that?"

I looked at him and said, "I wouldn't *like* to do that, but I'm willing to do that." I went on to explain that most of my friends around the world can't "dress up" to be accepted in places of worship, but I would do whatever was necessary for their voices to be heard through the things I came to say.

The dean looked at me and, in sincere humility, thanked me for coming and told me that he was fine with the clothes I had.

DAVID, GOLIATH AND SAUL'S ARMOR

This sort of thing seemed to happen a lot in the history of Israel. In 1 Samuel 17, the Scriptures tell us of one particular instance. The Philistines, a military aristocracy who emerged in Palestine around the same time as Israel, "gathered their forces for war" (verse 1). They were trying to secure trade routes from inland to the sea, so we see throughout the book of Judges the struggle to control the area of Palestine called the Shephelah.

Determined to win, the Philistines sent their champion Goliath, a big boy who stood nearly ten feet tall, to the front of the battle line as their delegate in a representative warfare scenario.[9] For forty days the giant Goliath taunted the Israelites, challenging them to send a champion for a one-on-one duel to settle the battle. Scripture tells us that "whenever the Israelites *saw* the man, they all fled from him in great fear" (verse 24). The Israelites saw with their eyes, and it blinded their hearts.

Along came David, a shepherd boy delivering grain, bread and cheese to his older brothers who were part of Israel's army. David showed up just about the time of day when Goliath would come out and bump his gums at the Israelites. David was offended. He was also surprised that no one had the courage to face this uncircumcised menace. So he volunteered to fight the giant.

King Saul was worried. None of his warriors had the courage to face Goliath. What made this little boy so confident? David proclaimed his faith, telling stories of how God had saved him from lions and bears. Perhaps in an exhausted act of desperation, Saul conceded and enlisted this young boy to fight the giant.

Saul's first move was to dress David up in the king's armor. Not a good fit. David put the sword and the traditional battle gear aside and simply started picking up little stones from a tiny brook. Then he took a staff, and off he went.

Sling shot, staff and a sack of five stones is all David had to fight Goliath. The Scriptures tell us that Goliath was armed and dressed to fight—in fact, just the head of one of his spears weighed fifteen pounds. Face to face they stood. Goliath suddenly had a problem with his vision: "He *looked* David over and saw that he was little more than a boy" (verse 42). Goliath was insulted—apparently he thought pretty highly of himself.

Anyway, if you know the story, David pops old Goliath in the head with a single stone from his slingshot and kills the giant. One shot and the battle was finished.[10]

Sometimes I think about David. I don't think he liked dressing up either. Before he became king he was a shepherd, and from what I understand, shepherds don't have strict dress codes. Sometimes I feel the church wants to dress me up in its clothes—clothes that don't fit and clothes that are pretty uncomfortable. David wanted to fight Goliath in his own threads. I like that. It worked for him. Worked real well. It works for me too.

Why does it seem that so many aspects of spirituality have to fit into certain molds? In noble efforts to catch and keep our attention, Christians have gimmicked out the Gospel by offering us formulaic approaches to cultivating our spirituality. Certain prayer practices, evangelical expectations and forms of personal devotions often leave us confused or wanting and needing more. It can get pretty complicated sometimes.

Jesus kept it simple. He actually dressed down—leaving the right hand of God and clothing himself in humanity. Jesus' teachings were simple too. Even little kids could understand them. He used everyday illustrations to explain the mysteries and secrets of the kingdom of God. But it seems we always complicate that too. Maybe Bono was right when he said, "Religion often gets in the way of God."[11]

FIVE SMALL STONES

Once I was in the checkout line at a grocery store in California, the day before leading a retreat for a college group. A headline on one of the tabloids in the checkout aisle caught my attention. I swear it read, "Goliath Was Shot with a .38!"[12]

Now, I was a theology major in college with an ancient biblical languages minor, and I don't remember anything in the Hebrew Scriptures concerning handguns. I was intrigued. I am embarrassed to admit it, but I bought that tabloid and read the article—twice.

Apparently, some archaeologist examined Goliath's skull (who knew they found his skull?) and determined that he was shot in the head with a gun—maybe even a semi-automatic rifle. The theory is based on what appears to be an exit wound in the back of the skull. There are even some experts who believe that it was a drive-by shooting: David was in a moving chariot when he fired the weapon. The article concludes with a hint of an ancient conspiracy theory, that maybe there was a second shooter.

I didn't take the article seriously, but it threw me off just enough to look at the David and Goliath story a little bit differently. Goliath was standing in the way of God's people moving into the Promised Land. No one was brave enough to fight him. In a serendipitous twist of events, David showed up and volunteered to take him on. We are told that David took five stones from the Brook of Elah and placed one in a slingshot to slay the giant (1 Samuel 17:49).

It's funny that David took five stones when the story indicates that he used only one of them. Was David that bad of a shot? Was there a mountain lion or something else harassing his flock that he was getting a few extra stones for? Had one of his older brothers played a prank on him, and did David need a stone or two to pop his brother's knee cap in revenge? Assuming all the little details in the Bible are infused with some sort of meaning, why five stones?

Over the years, I've read different biblical scholars' interpretations of the symbolism in the details. For instance, some believe that the five stones represented the pentapolis, or the five cities of Canaan (Ashdod, Ashkelon, Ekron, Gath and Gaza) that David would ultimately conquer. On the other hand, rabbinic tradition speculates that Goliath had four other brothers who were also giants that David would need to fight as they sought vengeance for their slain brother, and the stones were reserved for each of them.[13]

Years ago I lived in Jerusalem to study archaeology and Hebrew. On one of the many field trips, I found myself standing on the dry banks of the same stream that David once stood upon. At that place, I bent down and collected five small, smooth stones and slipped them into my backpack. When I returned from Israel, I put them in my dresser and forgot about them. Years later, as I was reflecting on my struggles to cultivate my spirituality, I took those stones out of my dresser, set them on my desk, and asked God what giants in my life were blocking my view of what God had in mind for me. I began to name them:

- *Pride* and *arrogance*
- *Individualism* and *independence*
- *Intemperance* and *excess*
- *Power* and *control*
- *Triumphalism, defiance* and *resistance*

I asked God to help me fight my giants. God gave me small stones of hope and promise, simple yet profound:

- *Humility* to slay the giant of *pride* and *arrogance.*
- *Community* to slay the giant of *individualism* and *independence.*
- *Simplicity* to slay the giant of *intemperance* and *excess.*
- *Submission* to slay the giant of *power* and *control.*
- *Brokenness* to slay the giant of *triumphalism, defiance* and *resistance.*

These five simple stones are central among the nine core values of Word Made Flesh. We call them our *Lifestyle Celebrations.* As I pray for the grace to live into a spirituality that embodies these simple commitments, I invite you to join me.

Writing on spirituality is a daunting endeavor. It seems to imply a sense of accomplishment. Well, I have a confession to make: I've hardly arrived anywhere. I'm much more a fanatic or activist than I am a contemplative or mystic. My spirituality has been expressed much more in my relationships, active life and cerebral ponderings than in the sacred, tranquil spaces of the heart and soul. Hopefully I'm stumbling forward in all of it, but spirituality is a language that I'm still learning to speak. I've not mastered it. Far from it. Its nuances and rhythms are still a mystery to me. These pages are a confession of that—more questions than answers.

As you read this book, I hope your eyes will be opened to the truth that the spirituality God wishes for us is really quite simple: that against humility, community, simplicity, submission and even brokenness no giant can stand, but only the God who delivers us from them into the promises found in Scripture.

1. HUMILITY

As I waited to sit with Mother Teresa for the first time, my mind was churning through a list of questions. I kept thinking that I needed to come up with the one question that no one had ever asked her—I wanted her to notice me and remember me.

As though a gentle breeze brushed my face, she suddenly and quietly appeared. Strength and meekness held in perfect tension, sitting beside me, she tenderly took my hands and set them in her lap.

Before I could even get a question past my lips, she looked straight into my eyes and started asking me about my family, my home, why I was in India. In mere moments she had set my heart at peace and made me feel as if I were the most important person in the world. Somehow in her busy schedule, she had time to sit with a college kid from Omaha, to get inside my head and heart. I felt sincerely loved by her.

I sat waiting for Mother Teresa in my yearning for significance, hoping to prove that I was different. Mother allowed herself to fade into the background and pressed me forward. Her grace demonstrated the truth that in God we are all beautiful and lovable. But this truth is something ascribed, not earned. Simple, obedient, loving, humble, Mother exposed the pride in me.

What is humility? Where does it come from? How do we find it? Humility is a principle and a virtue that flows from love in its purest form. It may even be the central virtue in Christianity—the true test of our true love. Francois de Salignac de La Mothe Fenelon puts it this way: "All the saints are convinced that sincere humility is the foundation of all virtues. . . . The more we love purely, the more perfect is our humility."[1]

Humility affirms our need for God. It is required to approach God. The Scriptures tell us that when we humble ourselves before the Lord, God will lift us up (James 4:10). Humility produces obedience as a sign and symbol of our love for God. Likewise, humility "is not concerned with one's own advantage but with that of others."[2] It's an obvious prerequisite for authentic community.

I have kicked myself countless times for starting this book with a chapter on humility. Humility is a hard one for me. As central to our faith, it's the most daring conversation to enter, lest pride trip you up at any discovery or conclusion. There are plenty of stories in the Scriptures that, if read through the lens of humility, open our eyes to new and simple insights. For example, consider how Jesus' disciples saw him in John 21:4-7.

The story takes place on the shores of the Sea of Galilee shortly after the resurrection of Christ. John writes, "Early in the morning, Jesus stood on the shore, but the disciples did not realize it was Jesus." Then Jesus calls out, "Friends, haven't you any fish?" They don't. The guys have been out all night working and have come up short. They let this stranger on the beach know he's out of luck too.

Jesus, still unrecognized, tells the guys to put their nets on the other side of the boat. They do and hit the jackpot. It is finally after the miraculous catch of fish that John exclaims, "It is the Lord!"

The disciples spent three years in ministry with Jesus. They were eyewitnesses to some of the most amazing events in history. They saw blind eyes opened, leprosy cured, physical disabilities healed, even the demon-possessed delivered. They saw a meager lunch of fish and bread feed thousands. They saw Jesus walk on water. It seems a foregone conclusion that if anyone would recognize Jesus, it would be his closest companions. But as the story tells us, after seeing Jesus and even hearing his voice, the disciples still didn't know who Christ was.

This story challenges me to evaluate how well I think I recognize the presence of Christ in my own life. I often convolute the simplicity of seeing Jesus. I'm usually pretty slow in waking up to the reality that Christ is near.

Being slow on the uptake is, in many ways, normal to the human condition. For example, I'm not the best version of myself early in the morning—and by "early in the morning" I mean before 10:00 a.m. It takes me a while to wake up. After twelve years of a beautiful marriage, I can always recognize my sweet wife Phileena in the wee hours of the morning, but recognizing the difference between right and left shoe isn't exactly something I've nailed down just yet. (I've also been known to slip my boxers on backwards—not good.)

In my spiritual awakening I often think I can distinguish the voice of God from the thoughts in my head. I think I recognize the difference between trials as spiritual distractions and trials as divine discipleship providing ongoing opportunity for me to grow. But I miss Jesus when I try to conform him to my image of what I want him to be.

It's humility that opens our eyes to the discovery of God. The self-righteous seem to have the hardest time recognizing God. Story after story in the Gospels illustrates this. The religious leaders and the disciples often misunderstood the identity of Jesus. At one point, the religious leaders accused Jesus of being the devil (Matthew 12:22-24).

The unrighteous, those more naturally in touch with their limitations, often seem to immediately recognize Jesus for who he is. The first recorded words from the man possessed by the legion of demons, for example, are: "What do you want with me, Jesus, Son of the Most High God?" (Luke 8:28). Something that Jesus' disciples discovered only gradually and the religious authorities of the day never realized—that Jesus was God in the flesh—was intuitively grasped by this marginalized victim of demonic oppression.

Perhaps those on the margins, the unrighteous and people who live in poverty—those familiar with humiliation—can see purity more clearly through their unpretentious "impurity." Perhaps they can see God's love through their own recognized need to receive love. Perhaps they can see Christ's unconditional acceptance through their experience with rejection. Perhaps we have something to learn from their humility.

When our pride gets in the way, the face of Jesus can be elusive when we expect him to mirror our version of Christianity rather than the kingdom reality he embodies. The challenge is to approach Jesus humbly, to take ownership of our inadequacies, weaknesses and needs. Humility is ultimately an issue of intimacy.

INTIMACY: SEEING GOD

How well do I really know God? I recently picked up a book that I had hoped would provoke my imagination regarding the virtue of humility. Sadly, the authors boiled down the need for humility to three easy motivational formulas. It's the sort of stuff that reminds me of spells and voodoo, as if one of the great spiritual journeys of all time could be condensed into a few easy steps. The authors suggested that humility must be cultivated first because we're told to—it's commanded of us. Second, we'd better be afraid of the consequences of our pride. Third, we will get rewarded if we're humble because God blesses the humble of heart.[3]

So it's that easy? We fulfill a duty so that we can rest assured that the fires of hell aren't a part of our future and can start counting our blessings early since we're promised a reward? It doesn't add up to me. It reminds me of the best of the worst of bumper sticker theologies. Have you seen the one that reads, "Flatter Jesus or He'll Torture You in Hell"? Wow. Really? So that's how he rolls?

Frequently I check myself: If there were no threat of hell and no promise of heaven, would I still serve God? I mean, what's the motivation if there's no punishment or reward in the equation? All I have to do to find the answer to this is pop open the Scriptures and start reading about a God who loves people who are poor, provides for them, honors them, seats them with princesses and princes. I *want* to serve and love a God who's so compassionate and kind, one who so generously loves, one who secures justice for my friends.

I celebrate these traits of God. The God who invites us into fellowship and communion, never imposing on our will but offering us love with an invitation to love back, has moved me from a fear-based faith to a relationship where intimacy is central.

How do we truly celebrate an authentic intimacy with God? For me it started with evaluating my vision of God.

LEARNING TO LOVE GOD

In the classic *Your God Is Too Small,*[4] J. B. Phillips presents constructive and destructive views of God that are often shaped during our childhood. Among the more popularly accepted destructive views of God are the "Resident Policeman," the "Parental Hangover," the "Grand Old Man," the "Meek and Mild," the "Managing Director," the "Perennial Grievance," the "Pale Galilean," and so on. These caricatures of God portray God as vindictive, overly punitive, controlling, detached and distant, reserved, micromanaging or nagging.

Growing up in an evangelical Christian home, I was introduced to a very familiar, very informal God. I was culturally conditioned to perceive God as "on demand" and at my beck and call. Songs like "What a Friend We Have in Jesus" only aggravated this comforting view of Christ. But even with a "friend" or "brother" in Jesus, I lived in mortal fear of missing the rapture. I can remember having to climb up on the counters to get the peanut butter jar down from the kitchen cabinets (I was a scrawny little kid). I worried that if I was left behind in the rapture I'd live life one slip away from breaking my neck every time I needed to eat. But worse than that, cooking for me meant dropping a couple Pop-Tarts in the toaster. If I ever got left behind, I was afraid I'd starve to death.

Hell was a completely different fear altogether. I've got to be honest, I didn't want to burn forever and ever. Sure, worms eating away at my soul is a pretty terrifying thought, but I'm funny about smells and the thought of smelling burnt hair just sets me off.

So eventually I caved into my fear and "got saved" from hell and from the possibility of scavenging for boxes of Pop-Tarts and jars of peanut butter.

It took me years to realize that "getting saved" out of fear isn't really salvation. I opened the Scriptures and stopped reading them as a threat and started finding Someone beautiful hidden in their pages. Suddenly there was this God who cares for those in need—I mean, really cares for them. Sure, the familial reading of God expressed in my Christian tradition loved me plenty, but God also deeply loved those who are poor. This God protected the vulnerable and defended the defenseless. I discovered a heavenly Father who gives good gifts to the children.

Pretty soon I was falling in love with a God that I had formerly domesticated and turned into my servant. I was scandalized by a caring Master tenderly valuing the servants.

As I learned to love God, my love was not motivated by fear or the threat of hell (not even by the promise of paradise), but rather by the character of the One who is by nature lovable. Christ was irresistible to me. I couldn't help but love Jesus the more I discovered who he was. The deeper I fell in love with God, the more I wanted to demonstrate that love.

As I became less familiar with God and more awed by God, intimacy naturally led me to obedience. That's what the Scriptures tell us. If we love God, then we'll obey God. Pretty simple. To learn to love God, I first had to unlearn how I perceived God, to break down the corners I had mentally backed God into. This journey continues today. My friends and I at Word Made Flesh continue to ask the questions, "How can we really see Jesus?" and "How can we selflessly learn to love Christ?"

It is in our intimate relationships with people who are poor, or more accurately our friends *who happen to be poor*, that our tainted views of God are transformed. It is our intimate relationships with our friends on the streets or in red-light districts that open our blinded eyes to really see Jesus for who he is. Through their desperation and forced vulnerability, they help us see what intimacy with God looks like. We are compelled to follow our friends who are poor to God's heart.

CHRIST WITH A COST

The closer we get to Christ, however, the more "dangerous" he becomes—dangerous to our attempts to control him or to limit his influence in our daily lives or even to domesticate him in the destructive prototypes that J. B. Phillips so articulately details for us.

A few years ago, Phileena and I visited the oldest bull ring in the world, in Seville, Spain. We bought tickets and sat in the summer sun taking in all the pageantry of the event. The matadors, splendidly dressed, pranced throughout the ring, enticing the bulls to spar.[5] I'm sure the bull fights were very controlled and I'm sure the real danger to the matadors was limited by a number of safety-mechanisms built in to protect the bull fighters; still it felt like a dangerous situation. Any contrived theatrics to elevate the adrenalin level of the spectators worked, and we watched in anticipation for the outcome of each fight.

I wonder if there is a correlation here to our spirituality. Do we act out a theatrical fight with God? Is it possible that we control the degree to which we seek intimacy with Christ by offering just enough of our personal will and freedoms to pacify God's desire to know us intimately? Do we really allow ourselves to draw close to the consuming nature of divine Lordship? Or are we practicing self-deception, acting out spiritual intimacy while keeping Jesus at a safe distance?

How intimate is our relationship with Christ? Intimate enough that all our programs for emotional happiness or preconceived perceptions of his identity or even our limited engagement with his control over us could be redeemed in us? That our love could be pure and selfless? That we would allow God to be God on God's terms?

BOWING OUR LIVES TO FIND GOD

There's a church in Bethlehem that was built to commemorate the birthplace of Christ. Since Bethlehem is only six miles south of Jerusalem, I visited the Church of the Nativity several times while I lived and studied there. They say that this gigantic, ornate church covers the stable where Jesus was born. It's a little unsettling to see what we have done to the simplicity of Jesus' life.

Anyway, it's believed that the actual spot of Christ's birth is in the basement of the church. It's covered in marble with a golden star in the center of the floor. To visit this spot you have to enter through this tiny little door. I'm not exactly tall (I like to think of myself as "fun size"), but it's pretty small even for me. It was intentionally designed so that to pass through it you must bow down. Visitors are forced to approach God in a posture of humility.

Humility is not a means to an end. Rather humility is the door through which we must enter to be welcomed into God's presence.

COMING UP SHORT

What can we really know about humility? I imagine any sensible person would agree that humility is elusive to us all. Humility is like the slipperiest fish in the tank: once you think you finally get your hands on it, you've lost it. Archbishop Desmond Tutu says:

> Humility is not pretending you don't have gifts. Sometimes we confuse humility with a false modesty that gives little glory to the One who has given us the gifts. Humility is the recognition that who you are is a gift from God and so helps you to sit reasonably loosely to this gift. This lessens the likelihood of arrogance because the recognition that our abilities and talents are gifts reminds us that they are not wholly ours and can be taken away. If we truly exulted in our gifts, we would also celebrate the gifts of other people and the diversity of talents that God has given all of us.[6]

I've often mistaken humility for modesty and even forms of self-disgust. False pride is another deformation of humility that has tricked me more than once. For a long time I even thought of humility in terms of humiliation—something that resembled humility at a distance, but smelled of pride the closer I got to understanding it.

I think for most of my faith journey, I've not known how to relate to humility because I've not known how to relate to God. My pride clouds my vision of God and ultimately myself.

This has been the struggle from before the beginning of time. We're told that pride was the potion that turned the angel Lucifer into the devil, Satan. He was beautiful. That's not bad—even the self-awareness of it. However, ambition (which isn't always a bad thing) pressed Lucifer to challenge his view of God, view of self and, in the end, his view of others.

It's scary to think that pride could be so powerful, so destructive. If an angel in God's presence had a hard time with pride, then what makes me think I can overcome it?

In the Gospels there's a story where all the guys are gathered talking about who will be the greatest (Matthew 18:1-5). If you stop and think about it, what they are really talking about is who is the most insecure. I mean, if you have to talk about how great you are, then aren't you really concerned that people don't have an accurate view of who you think you are? If you have to push yourself forward, isn't there a certain amount of fear that someone might be better than you in whatever it is you're trying to gain ground in?

Fear drives us to these places. Sometimes our real and deep needs to be accepted, esteemed, honored or loved make us want to promote ourselves.

I wonder what Christ must have been thinking as he listened to the guys talk about how great they are. It must have been some conversation. And you've got to love how Jesus handled it. I'm sure Jesus knew exactly what was in their hearts and minds. I wonder how long Christ let the conversation go on before he called a little kid over.

The story goes that as the disciples were talking themselves up, the Master centered a child and said, "Whoever wants to be the greatest needs to humble himself like this child." Classic.

I wish there was some back story on that kid. Did any of the disciples know him? Had he T.P.'ed any of their houses or broken any of their windows with antiquity's equivalent of a baseball? Had he dated any of their daughters and broken any of their hearts? Whoever this boy was, his prophetic presence silenced the men.

What I find funny about that story is that Jesus centered the child, not himself. Really. Jesus could have pointed to himself as the model of humility, but he chose a kid. Makes sense. Jesus put someone else forward.

This is how we find Christ—in the sincere desire to be completely surrendered to God in such a way that no emotional or mental safety mechanisms prevent God from showing us the divine character. This is the path to humility, to really love God, know God and be known by God.

UNIMPRESSING GOD

Several years ago Phileena and I were visiting some friends for dinner. They are a generous family that has often made great sacrifices to give to those in need. While we were on our way to their home, the family gathered the children for orientation on who Phileena and I were and what we did. As our friend explained to his children that Phileena and Chris "help feed the poor," their buzzed-hair and barrel-chested three-year-old son responded, "So! Do they feed the animals?"

That kid has the insight of a future spiritual director if I've ever met one. That boy wasn't impressed with what we do. In his world, animals needed help too, and if these so-called compassionate dinner guests were going to earn favor in his eyes, then we had better be pouring milk for cats and shoveling hay for elephants. Seriously. Like I said, the insight of a future spiritual director.

When I heard about the question he asked, it all came together. There is nothing we can be proud about in our obedience if it is truly a sign of our love for our heavenly Father. Whether it is serving among friends on the margins or feeding the animals, as long as what we do finds its basis in our love for God, then all the glory goes to God. Paul validates this when speaking of love: "If I give all I possess to the poor and surrender my body to the flames, but have not love, I gain nothing" (1 Corinthians 13:3). An ancient mystic put it this way: "The truly humble [are] perfectly obedient, because [they have] renounced [their] own will."[7]

For myself, obedience brought me to India. I moved to the edge of a slum and tried my best to be a good neighbor. I helped open a home for children with AIDS. It was an incredible time in my life.

But soon enough I fell back into the role of being my own personal redeemer, thinking that my efforts and noble deeds would earn me eternal extra-credit points.

It's God who asked that my love be a response to God's love for me. There's no way pride can enter the relationship unless what I presume to be acts of love are actually self-justifying, misguided efforts to save myself or to impress God. And guess what? God's not impressed, any more than my three-year-old friend. It wasn't that he had anything against me personally; he wasn't being a punk. He was onto the truth that God sees us as God's own, that we are "enough" just being ourselves before God. God's love is not like the world's version of love, which is predicated on resumes and awards and even benevolent actions; God sees our humility as a response to God's invitation to intimacy.

God's love makes it safe to approach God with humility. I bow my head, chin against my chest, back bent forward, and I affirm my need for a Creator, a Savior and a Redeemer. I also let myself imagine how much God must love me.

COMING FACE TO FACE

"Zacchaeus was a wee little man and a wee little man was he," or at least that's how the song goes. If you don't know the tune, count yourself blessed. Because of that song and its annoying ability to relentlessly embed itself in my mind, I never really took Zacchaeus very seriously. I mean, seeing the badly drawn flannel-graphs of this wee little man peeking out of a tree should have been enough to make me never forget his tale, but that goofy song . . .

I recently rediscovered Zacchaeus. In Luke 19:1-10, Jesus entered Jericho; Zacchaeus wanted to see him. But this guy was short. So up a tree he went to get a better view. Jesus looked up, saw Zacchaeus and not only asked him to get out of the tree but invited himself to Zacchaeus's home.

Something happened. Zacchaeus was transformed and promised to give half of everything he owned to his neighbors in need.
He pledged that he would make amends and repay all those he
had cheated. Jesus proclaimed, "Today salvation has come to this
house."

It's a simple story, actually pretty good material for a song.
There was an arrival—Jesus showed up. There was a perspective—
Zacchaeus climbed the tree. There was an invitation—they met face
to face. There was a response—Zacchaeus was transformed. Jesus
disarmed Zacchaeus's pride and wrapped that wee little man up in
humility.

It's counterintuitive. You would think that Zacchaeus would be
more familiar with humiliation than pride—I mean, after all, he was
short, despised (he worked for "the man" as a tax collector) and sin-
gled out for being up in a tree. But it's his pride that brought him
there. The imagery is easy to pick on. Zacchaeus was trying to get an
angle on Christ, but he didn't walk up to Jesus like a normal person.
He climbed high up in a tree, assuming a position of leverage.

Being fun-sized, I know what it is like to have to climb on something to get a better view. Fire hydrants, fences, park benches,
trees—you name it, I've climbed it. If there is something happening
and a crowd has gathered, then it is likely I am going to miss out on
the action unless there is something nearby to stand on.

I have something else in common with Zacchaeus. I want to see
Jesus. I want to figure out who he is. I try to get an "angle" on
Christ. I look for different points of view from where I can figure
out who Jesus is. I do things, go places, surround myself with the
right people or try and read the *right* books so I can be in a better
position to see Jesus—I climb my own sorts of trees. The things I
use to try to get a better view of Jesus always leave me frustrated
and empty.

Zacchaeus must have had a great view of Christ from that tree, but it wasn't the right view. It was a view that Zacchaeus controlled. To see Jesus, to really get a good look at him, we have to come face to face with him. It is the times when I come to Christ vulnerable that he really shows himself to me.

Because I know that God sees everything, I often pride myself in my own transparency before God. But transparency isn't vulnerability. I do a pretty good job of protecting myself in relationships. I'm open enough that I can get by without having to *need* anything from anyone. I would be humiliated by such weakness. But I'm finding that's a form of pride—and not even a deformed version of pride, just regular old pride.

It was recently pointed out to me that the word *vulnerable* comes from the Latin word for "wound." Therefore, to be *vulnerable* means to be capable of being wounded. So the trees I climb (missions experiences, conferences and retreats, books and relationships with the *right* people), and the tree Zacchaeus climbed, expose the real (and often hidden) need and desire to see God. And really, it's just another attempt to try and save ourselves.

I wonder if Jesus laughed a little bit seeing a short guy hanging on some branches. What must it have been like when their eyes met? I can imagine Jesus thinking, *Zacchaeus, that's my tree, not yours. And the time hasn't come, but I will climb it to save you.*

In the story, Jesus invites himself to Zacchaeus's home. A meal is implied; no good host in Zacchaeus's culture would allow a guest to get away without eating something. It's still like that in most places today. A meal isn't like the distant, impersonal connection (more like observation) that Zacchaeus was willing to settle for. A meal is much more intimate and personal. Christ humbled himself by sitting at the table. Face to face, he confronted the pride in a man who thought he could figure out Jesus from a distance. Christ pursued the wee little fun-size man. Christ ascribed dignity and validated his identity.

Once they were together, face to face, Zacchaeus was transformed. This newfound intimacy with Christ led to a newfound obedience, and before you know it Zacchaeus was settling debts and offering his wealth to those in need. The story ends with restoration and reconciliation. Zacchaeus was not the donor but the receptor. Zacchaeus wanted to see God, to know God. Jesus wanted to know Zacchaeus, to love him. Zacchaeus embraced that acceptance and began to understand God's love for the world, for his own neighbors in need. Admitting that he had done wrong and humbling himself before God, Zacchaeus no longer needed to put forward a false self.

All this foreshadows the cross, really. I try to see Jesus in so many ways, but it's only when I come face to face with him that I'm transformed. The things I try to climb up to see Christ are false crosses that I make for myself, hoping they'll save me. Jesus calls me down. From his cross, I learn to see his love for me. At his table he gives me the eyes to see his love for the world.

SEEING MY NEIGHBOR

In my free time while studying in Israel, I would wander around the Old City exploring the tiny passageways and the intricacies of ancient Jerusalem.

On one sunny afternoon, I found myself in the area of St. Stephen's gate, near the modern day site of the *Via Dolorosa*, the "path of suffering" where Jesus is thought to have carried his cross. At the end of the *Via Dolorosa* stood a Palestinian man. He had a long black beard and dirty hair that fell below his shoulders. His eyes were kind. He was barefoot. He had no pants. The only thing keeping him from being completely naked was the open rag of a shirt that he wore, torn and dirty, loosely hanging off his shoulders. It caught me off guard. He obviously was not in his right mind. However, this man was gentle. As his dazed eyes drifted into the sparsely clouded sky, I could tell he was harmless.

Various tour groups making their pilgrimages through Jerusalem would walk down this path with tears in their eyes and the typical romanticized holy-land-tour wistfulness. Arriving at the end of the path, the tour groups and pilgrims came face to face with this naked man. Their responses were usually very similar. At first, most were frightened by the man. Many flat out ignored him, walking right past him, acting as though he wasn't there. Some, realizing he was harmless and helpless, would cruelly try to scare him off or send him away.

I sat there most of the afternoon taking it all in, wondering how something so seemingly absurd could still happen in our world today.

I went back to my dorm room that evening and began reading through the Scriptures. I found myself stuck in Matthew 13:44, where a man discovers treasure—real, live hidden treasure—in a field. The passage tells us that "joyfully" he went off to sell all his possessions in order to buy the field. Pretty simple concept, but almost seems a little dishonest, doesn't it? Anyway, I sat at my desk, Bible open, thinking about the meaning of this verse.

That evening in Jerusalem, I felt like it made sense; it seemed simple. At first I thought it meant that I have to give up everything in order to get this kingdom, but I started to understand that there was more.

I was compelled to pray about the passage. Suddenly it was as if the Lord took a hold of my heart, trying to show me that I was the "hidden treasure." Jesus joyfully went to the cross and sold everything (his own life) so that I could be his. I was overcome with a sense of God's love for me. It broke me. I sat at my desk weeping, drinking in the love that God was lavishing, pouring out on me.

It was a discovery of humility. There was nothing I could do to attain "treasure status." It is something God ascribes and bestows. Even more than there not being anything I could do to be worthy of God's love, there also wasn't opportunity for me to beat myself up over it. I couldn't downplay my unworthiness or point out all the mistakes and flaws in my life to tarnish the treasure God saw in me. I was humbled in God's love.

I reflected on the events of that day, remembering the pain and sadness I saw reflected in the face of the naked man. Praying for that man, the Lord opened my eyes to the hidden treasure that had been standing before me. That crazy man, naked and dirty, also was a "hidden treasure" that Jesus loved so much that he gave his all for him. Joyfully, the Master sold everything in order that this man could be a part of the family of God. I was given the eyes to see the dignity in "the other." That demanded a response—of love, obedience.

Ironic that Christ met me that day as a naked man on the same path Jesus carried his own cross. Two thousand years earlier, King Jesus detailed the terms of the fateful day of judgment. The language he used communicated identification with the poor ("I was hungry, I was thirsty, I was a stranger, I needed clothes, I was sick, I was in prison . . ." Matthew 25:31-46). On that day when I found myself in Jerusalem, it was as if the King was there, presenting an opportunity to give to him through the needs of that hidden treasure yet to be discovered. Only discovered in the humility of learning to see Christ.

The King, Christ, surprised me. He wasn't dressed up in ornate robes but stood naked among the poor. Christ validated the divine imprint on humanity by showing me the treasure in that naked and vulnerable Palestinian man. Seeing my own value to God—a treasure hidden in my false self—was a lesson in humility. Seeing that man on the *Via Dolorosa* as a treasure equal in value to myself, waiting to be discovered, was a lesson in community.

2. COMMUNITY

It was a Saturday, the day that Nepali Christians observe the Sabbath, when Bhanu was arrested for standing up for her faith.

In the middle of the church service, several undercover policemen stood up and arrested everyone in the room. The congregation, stunned and afraid, was taken outside the home where they had gathered to worship. The police officers then brought the young believers to a statue of Buddha and demanded that every person bow before the statue and take the ceremonial chalk mark on their forehead, indicating that they had made their prayers. If the church members bowed before the Buddha they would be released and the charges would be dropped.

The first person in line bowed and took the mark on his forehead. The second followed by bowing. Nearly seventy Christians had already bowed before the idol when Bhanu, a sixteen-year-old girl, refused to lower her head. Immediately she was beaten and thrown to the ground. The police officers wanted to make an example of her. But her strength and dedication inspired her fellow parishioners. Ten people out of the entire congregation—the pastor, Bhanu and the last eight people in that line stood strong. They were taken to jail and in a miraculous turn of events were released in less than two weeks.

As a Nepali church-planter translated Bhanu's testimony for us,

Phileena and I were astonished. The simple act of defiance of a young girl in the face of persecution galvanized her identity in relation to her faith and challenged her own fellowship to deeper devotion. Her gift of courage was an example offered back to each of us. Her faith and perseverance shows the value community has in its ability to confer stability and potency in the body of Christ. Bhanu, standing with and for her community, testified that her identity was found in something greater than herself—her community.

IDENTITY AND ACCOUNTABILITY

Often, community provides orientation and clarification for identity. Both in intimate relationships such as marriage and in thriving and growing communities, who we are is accented and highlighted—the best of us and the worst of us.

Community also provides accountability. In community, sin cannot be isolated from others. When we are selfish or unresponsive to God, we have less to give to our community. When we fail to give or be present to our community, we not only hurt ourselves, we hurt those around us. Dietrich Bonhoeffer writes, "Sin wants to remain unknown. It shuns the light. In the darkness of the unexpressed it poisons the whole being of a person."[1] But in community, sin is exposed, and a place for confession and acceptance is born. An envelope of grace is established.

What we put into community is what we get out of it. Bhanu stood for Christ, and that stand was a grace to her and to us. For Western people this may be difficult to grasp. Most North American Christians view a church service more as a performance than as fellowship. We go to the churches that have the best worship, or the most stimulating preaching, or the best facilities. We can slip in on a Sunday morning, sing a few songs, maybe give something in the offering, hear a message that's spoken to or at us, and then leave without having to interact with anyone. Though a typical church service, this is not church. This is a production or presentation, and the churchgoer with this mentality becomes part of an audience instead of part of the body of Christ. Community provides blessing and nourishment when one invests in it and sacrifices for it. The sacrifice and love that we give is the blessing. That is why what we put into community is what we get out of it.

Bhanu and her friends paint a picture of the ideal that communities should aspire to: orientation and clarification about who we are—at our best and worst—and embodied accountability that points us toward who we could be. Bhanu's sacrifice wasn't in vain because her community was open to her witness. At its best, Christian community is the body of Christ, living and active in the world.

COMMUNITY CHANGED MY LIFE,
BUT LIFE CHANGED MY COMMUNITY

Our first impressions of how community works are in the form of tribalism: the homogenous people-groups, or tribes, we find ourselves in inspire an instinctive loyalty and construct our understanding of virtue. My first experiences in a community are found in the family I was born into—the good and bad of it, the joys and sorrows. Trying to find out who I was within the embrace of family prepared me to explore other entry points into community.

The Catholic elementary school I attended created other early ideas about community. Much more diverse than my family, yet still fairly homogenous, elementary school forced me to interact with people whom I might not otherwise have chosen to pursue.

My YMCA pee-wee league baseball and soccer teams taught me about communal loyalty—I learned to despise the other teams in their blue or green shirts. Such early patterns of overidentification were sadly reinforced by our team sponsor, a local bank who paid for our yellow shirts.[2] This notion of loyalty was malformed even more as I fell deeply in love with college football. Even today my college football fanaticism most clearly exposes my sins of tribalism.[3]

The youth group I attended in high school gave me some of my first involved encounters with religious community. Having a group of peers struggling with the same faith I was trying to sort out was not only comforting but inspiring.

College, especially living in the dorms, forged thoughts and experiences on shared life and offered my first communal experience outside my family life. My years at the university also exposed me to my need for community—a need that was quickly met by a group of six fellow students that helped me grow up. I had moved from Omaha to Kentucky, and my early feelings of displacement were shared by many other new students, and this drove us together. Our friendship and community was so deep that we actually tattooed a symbol representing it onto each of our ankles.

After graduation I joined the missional community Word Made Flesh and moved to South India. My assumptions on what community had been in my life up to that point were abruptly challenged.

My first neighborhood out of college was in Chennai (formerly Madras). It was unlike anything I had ever been exposed to. Christian, Hindu and Muslim neighbors took care of one another. Even now, years after moving away from that neighborhood, I still maintain deep and meaningful relationships with my friends there—relationships that I almost consider family.

A couple years later Phileena and I were married. Our marriage became a new and deeply intimate microcommunity. Suddenly every action I took and decision I made had an immediate and obvious impact on my wife. The negative consequences and positive benefits of my personal rhythms, ruts and disciplines (or lack thereof) were absorbed by this newly formed family of two.

Not long after we were married, Word Made Flesh suddenly reimagined itself, making community even more central to all our perceived ministry activities. The starting point was no longer activism but intimacy with God and one another. Everything changed, and I think we've all been recovering (as we're being restored) since then.

I'm now trying to figure out virtual community and identity as I try to keep up with MySpace and Facebook, where people post anything on public walls—even deeply personal and intimate statements they would never say to the owner of that wall over a cup of coffee. I wonder if this virtual environment is actually damaging the spirit of true community because it's actually more closely related to role-playing games.

When I was a little kid, my neighborhood was a lot like the one portrayed in the film *The Sandlot*. We had all sorts of kids come together almost daily for baseball or street football. Today the only space where many kids play football is on their PSP or Xbox, and even the most unathletic kid can accumulate mad stats by playing as Reggie Bush. These virtual surrogates for traditional venues for building relationships create the illusion that we can become whoever we want, by associating with virtual friends, causes, groups or organizations.

THE GRACE OF COMMUNITY

The sandlot, street football on North 77th ("the House of Pain," we called it) and authentic community have been graces in my life. Community has been a place of sorrow and celebration—these same hands have held and raised glasses of wine in times of joy, and wiped tears from my eyes after holding and burying friends who left too soon. The friends around me have guided me through my darkest days of loneliness, doubt, fear and insecurity. My worst sins have been confessed in community, and the love I've found there has given me the courage to receive real forgiveness.

As a grace, community has also created some of the deepest wounds in my heart. Unfair or failed expectations, hard words, misunderstandings, betrayal, accusations, disappointments, even lone-liness in community—I remember hearing someone say that commu-nity is wherever the people you least want to be with always live.

All of these things have never been very far removed from any of my community experiences. Though I need community more than any other discipline, it has been one of the hardest things for me to find my way in. With as much work that needs to go into com-munity, and as hard and painful as it has been working it out, why in the world would I choose it?

I choose community because that's where I've found God. Who we are cannot be separated from relationships. We were made for relationships.

THE MIRROR OF COMMUNITY

Examining *who* we are begins with understanding dignity and iden-tity. Chris Sugden and Vinay Samuel analyze this language and its implications. Dignity is an issue of *value* and identity is an issue of *substance*. "Identity answers the question 'Who am I?', while dignity answers the question 'What am I worth?'"[4]

"Dignity and identity depend on a truly biblical doctrine of [hu-manity]."[5] This fact is foundational to all discussions about dignity and identity. The worth of a person is directly related to the fact that he or she is created in the image of God. John Stott sees in "the divine image in [humanity] . . . an intrinsic dignity or worth, a worth which belongs to all human beings."[6] That dignity can seem-ingly be tarnished by the bad decisions we make, but by its very nature it can't be challenged. Likewise, people who are poor may live in undignified circumstances, but their intrinsic dignity can't be contested; they are, according to Leonardo and Clovis Boff, the "disfigured image of God."[7]

"While identity must not be confused with dignity, dignity in a Christian view assumes identity."[8] In the empire of humanity, talk of what we *are* points to what we are *worth*. If we have an impressive education, a good job, a nice home, a lot of money, a sweet ride or if we think we are attractive, then—it seems to us—we are worth more. In this empire, being worth more makes us more valuable. We then use terms that imply meanings of popularity, beauty and strength, all of which mean that we are approved and accepted by those around us.

In the upside-down kingdom of God, by contrast, what we are *worth* points to who we *are*. If we can view God as a Father, that makes us his children; if God is a king, that makes us princes and princesses. The Scriptures tell us that God is a king, and theology bears that out: an omnipotent God is sovereign by default. The Scriptures go on, however, to tell us that God is our Father. Rather than being subjects of a despot, we are princes and princesses of the King of kings. All this, the Scriptures tell us, is by the ministry of Christ, who gave his life so that we might call the sovereign God Father. We learn that in the eyes of God, we are worth the life of the One who gives us life; God views every person who has ever lived as worth shedding blood for, worth dying for. We are worth the suffering of our King.

In other words, our dignity comes from God, allowing our identity to be found in God.

The empire of humanity asserts dignity and identity as something that must be earned. Participating in the empire of humanity then becomes an ongoing struggle to do the right things, to have the right things, to be the right kind of person. The kingdom of God, however, ascribes dignity and identity freely, even if it is not consciously accepted. *Being* is valued over *doing*, *giving* is valued over *having*, and all the right things need not be sought after but only accepted as they are freely available to God's children.

The differentiation between these two kingdoms is crucial to note. In the kingdom of God, dignity and identity conclusively are not earned but ascribed through a right relationship with the King. The Scriptures instruct us to "seek first God's Kingdom" and *then* "all these things will be given to you" (Matthew 6:33). If we are more caught up in seeking to claim our true dignity and identity than we are in seeking God, we will never find either. Finding and claiming these things comes first through knowing Jesus. Effort spent looking to discover who we are apart from Christ is misguided, and the energy spent is misplaced.

As individuals, we find ourselves pinned between these kingdoms. We erroneously apply the principles of the world to our relationship with God—to *do* so that we can *be*. We think that we need to do the right things to earn God's love and acceptance. We think that we have to earn our place in God's family. However impossible that is, for many, seeking to earn this approval is much easier than simply receiving the approval that is already available.

Four Distinctions Between the Empire of Humanity and the Kingdom of God

The Empire of Humanity	*The Kingdom of God*
What we are points to what we are worth.	What we are worth validates who we are.
Seeking dignity and identity is an endless pursuit for false validation.	Seeking God brings completion.
Dignity and identity must be earned.	Dignity and identity are ascribed.
Dignity and identity are achieved by *doing*.	Dignity and identity come by *being*.

Henri J. M. Nouwen, recognizing that the path to embracing our identity is obstructed with deception, identified three lies that need to be overcome in order to know that we are beloved daughters and sons of God.[9]

I AM WHAT I HAVE

First, "I am what I have." This statement holds much power over us.

When we have nice things, we feel good about ourselves. When we don't have nice things, and sometimes when we don't have the *nicest* things, we feel discontented and unfulfilled. Samuel Kamaleson, former vice president at-large for World Vision International, often refers to the *nonvalues* of the kingdom of God. One of these *nonvalues* is possessions. Kamaleson explains that if we are unable to give something away, then we do not *possess* it, rather it *possesses* us.

In a culture saturated with overconsumption and gross materialism, it is hard not to believe this lie. The empire of humanity teaches us to live above our means, obtaining things that we are unable to afford and living lifestyles that are not sustainable. So we spend more money to make ourselves feel better. Or we work harder and save more money so that our bank-account balances will provide us with a false sense of security. We make sure that our company provides us with the best retirement plan so that when we're old we can have "enough" to be comfortable. We study to earn degrees, thinking they will define us and increase our marketable worth to the world. We try to keep up with the latest in fashion and entertainment so that we don't get "left behind." We move from one house to another, seeking out the bigger and better, all the while making sure that where we live is in the "right" part of town or in the "right" neighborhoods. We work hard to get ahead. The titles and positions are never enough, and so we sacrifice everything to move up the social or occupational ladder, desperately trying to "arrive." We give up who we truly are to try to become something we will never be. This becomes a habitual and destructive way of living. We're never free to celebrate what we have because we're always looking for what we can get and what we think we want or need.

Beyond that, however, the lie "I am what I have" is so individualized, so self-centered, that we're left without room for the voice and participation of community.

"I am what I have" doesn't just affect us; it destroys the dignity and identity of our friends who suffer. The Basque Jesuit Jon So-brino suggests that people who celebrate consumerism and mate-rialism "ignore how such an attitude has fostered insensibility to-ward the human community and even encouraged selfishness and aloofness."[10] Our view of poverty becomes defined not by access to resources or opportunity but by possessions. Non-poor Christians mistakenly come to view God's financial and material provision as individual blessing rather than kingdom resources. We work not for justice for everyone but instead to ensure that we're on the "right" side of the poverty line.

Sobrino writes, "The causes of sufferings in the [Majority World] are, to a great extent, to be found in the First World. To admit this is a necessary condition for the First World to know itself truthfully. Deciding to remove this suffering is essential if the First World is to carry out its fundamental ethical responsibility. To actually do away with this suffering is the way of salvation for both [Major-ity] and First World."[11] Honestly, sometimes I just read right over or through statements like that. What does that mean for me?

A movie called *Traffic* helped me understand how bridges are built. In the movie, high school students partying on the weekends in Cincinnati help to create orphans and widows in Mexico City. These students buy drugs that are manufactured in and trafficked from Mexico. However, poverty creates a trap, and the people in-volved in the supply chain of the drug ring feel they have no other opportunity that would secure adequate income for their families. The Mexicans involved in the drug trafficking put themselves in an extremely vulnerable scenario that is marked by addiction, violence and fear.

God uses those who are poor as a standard for judgment (see Matthew 25). If our community makes no room for those who are poor, our community loses all credibility. Sobrino challenges us to recover our true dignity and identity in order to clarify the dignity and identity of our friends on the margins, which allows for the possibility of community to happen.

I AM WHAT OTHER PEOPLE SAY ABOUT ME

The second lie, according to Nouwen, is "I am what other people say about me." So many of us see ourselves through the eyes of others. We compare ourselves to the world around us and submit ourselves to the world's critique. When people say good things about us, we have a good day. When people say bad or negative things about us, we have a bad day. Soon the good things go unheard. We clothe ourselves with a false humility by brushing aside compliments and encouragement, only hoping that the deflection of the praise or affirmation will invite more of the same.

I once gave a chapel message at a Christian college in which I focused on understanding our true dignity and identity. During the course of the presentation I shared some of my assumptions about the church's role in causing poverty. Many seemed to be moved by my message, but some took offense at my comments. The days following that presentation were difficult for me as I kept repeating the criticisms to myself.

When our sense of dignity and identity is based on what other people say, we can be emotionally scarred, sometimes for life, by the negative and hurtful comments people make. When we hear criticism, negativity, disappointment we may have caused and reprimanding voices, we fall victim to them and our self-perception is damaged.

Jesus lived with criticism. Jesus' stand for justice invited it, even invited corresponding persecution. The negative words, false accusations and unfair judgments levied against him only strengthened his witness. Jesus knew who he was and to whom he belonged. The words of those around him did not affect his self-understanding but showed more clearly the false identities of his accusers.

Jürgen Moltmann writes, "By proclaiming the righteousness of God as the right of those who were rejected and without grace to receive grace, he provoked the hostility of the guardians of the law. By becoming a 'friend of sinners and tax-collectors,' he made their enemies his enemies. By claiming that God . . . was on the side of the godless, he incited the devout against him and was cast out into the godlessness of Golgotha."[12]

Christ's siding with "the other" made him a target for unfair and untrue accusations. His example stands for us today. When we absorb the negative things that people say of us—whether they're true or false—we fall victim to Nouwen's second lie. We can and must look to Christ. Jesus heard the criticisms and accusations, yet he maintained a quiet and deep confidence that he was the beloved. Could we find that quiet confidence, allowing ourselves to be free from the pains and fears of what people say about us?

I AM WHAT I DO

The third lie that Nouwen refers to is "I am what I do." For many of us, the things we fill our time with become not so much expressions of who we are but rather distractions from whom we need to become. I perpetually find myself falling into this lie, thinking that because I'm part of a missional community God approves of me.

I am afraid of the inner voice that speaks to me of my dignity and identity. I am afraid to confront the failures of my past and the disappointments yet to be experienced in my future. I look at the bad things I've done and am ashamed, and so I fill my days with activities to distract me. I fill my ears with music to keep me from facing God's tender voice calling me. I fill my eyes with images to subdue the restless activity of my mind. All of this to avoid the hurts of my past and the shame of my present. Sometimes I even fill my time with community activities to fill up the space that actually belongs to God.

"I am what I do" can dehumanize us. When we look at our past successes and accomplishments, we can feel good about ourselves. When we look at our past failures and disappointment, we can beat ourselves up and destroy the belovedness that we must learn to claim.

When we don't know who we are, we are unavailable to be given to the world around us. Jean Vanier writes, "So many of us flee from people crying out in pain, people who are broken. We hide in a world of distraction and pleasure or in 'things to do.' We can even hide in various groups of prayer and spiritual exercises, not knowing that a light is shining in the poor, the weak, the lonely and the oppressed."[13]

The things we do, even the good things, can become illusions that perpetuate a false identity of who we see ourselves as. Arriving at a place where we are able to claim kingdom dignity and identity propels us to secure that truth for others. As simple as it is difficult, we must learn to see past the lies "I am what I have," "I am what I do," and "I am what other people say about me" to the truth that we are the beloved sons and daughters of the King. Seeing our own belovedness will give us the eyes to see the belovedness of others. Learning to recognize these truths about ourselves allows us to see these things for and in our community. It creates the space for the miracle of community to happen.

COMMUNITY FOR ACCOUNTABILITY

It was a Monday afternoon, and several of us—Word Made Flesh staff Josh Tucker, field director Sarah Lance, Phileena and I—were on our way to Sonagachi, one of South Asia's most notorious red-light districts. As we were walking to the subway station, we almost stumbled over an emaciated body lying on the sidewalk. The little person was underneath a dirty blanket covered with what must have been a thousand flies. From underneath the blanket and body, a three-foot trail of diarrhea ran toward the gutter.

It's not uncommon to see bodies lining the streets of Kolkata, but even after many years of exposure to such injustice and disregard for humanity, I am still shocked by it.

My pal Josh tapped the body on the shoulder to see if the person was dead. The body moved. Josh pulled the blanket down from the face that it covered to see a helpless young man, maybe twenty-two years old and visibly stunned by our approach. As soon as he realized we were there to help him, he began weeping uncontrollably. A crowd gathered. He continued to cry.

We didn't have much to work with, but our friend Sarah grabbed a bottle of water and some newspaper. She began cleaning the young man, wiping the diarrhea off with the newspaper and rinsing him with the water. We asked him his name. Tutella Dhas. He was lost, afraid, alone. His body was a leathery-skinned skeleton, and his bulging eyes accentuated the shape of his skull. He kept crying.

We tried to get a taxi, but none would stop. The crowd grew. No one wanted to help. Two more friends happened to be walking down the street just then, and they were able to find a taxi. They took Tutella Dhas with them and headed off to Mother Teresa's House for the Dying. Phileena, Sarah, Josh and I stood there in disbelief.

I lifted my head and caught sight of a church and its sign less than five feet from where we found the dying Tutella Dhas. The sign read, "All are welcome here." It may have been what inspired someone to drop Tutella in front of the church. But was he welcome? People from the church watched as we helped Tutella, yet the gate remained closed.

If all were truly welcome, then why was a man dying at the threshold of the church? Why didn't anyone come out to help him?

The closed church gate reflects my own closed heart and our closed Christian communities. The sign welcomes the Lord, but the door is tightly shut. We want to let God in, but usually on our terms. We want to make room for Christ to reign on the thrones of our hearts, but only a clean Christ who doesn't make a mess of our lives.

When the church wants to justify itself, it often fills the image of Christ with values that don't resemble those of Jesus of Nazareth. However, as Jon Sobrino says, "Christ without Jesus of Nazareth is a fantastic abstraction."[14]

Who was this Jesus of Nazareth? He was a poor man who lived in community among peasants. He formed an unlikely community that changed the world. Jayakumar Christian, the head of World Vision India, reflects on the Jesus of Nazareth with a series of contradictions.

- He was born in a manger, not a palace.
- The news of his birth was announced to shepherds and not princes.
- When he formed his ministry team, he chose fishermen, not seminarians.
- He ministered in Galilee, not in Rome.
- He rode into Jerusalem on a donkey and not a stallion.
- He died like a criminal, hung between two thieves, on a cross.[15]

The Gospels report that Jesus of Nazareth had no place to lay his head (Luke 9:58). The Scriptures tell us he was a man of sorrows. There was nothing about his appearance that made him desirable. He was rejected by humanity (Isaiah 53:2-3).

Jesus of Nazareth wasn't the insipid, pale-white, blue-eyed Jesus of Sunday school flannel-graph boards. His power was found in powerlessness. Jesus of Nazareth became poor so that through his poverty the world could become rich (2 Corinthians 8:9). He chose those who are poor in the eyes of the world to receive the riches of faith (James 2:5). He even used examples of our responsiveness to our sisters and brothers in need to illustrate his kingdom's standard of judgment (Matthew 25:31-46).

Is this the Jesus I welcome in my heart? Is this Jesus welcomed in our churches? Do our communities recognize Christ and his needs when he so kindly and unexpectedly offers them to us? Could this Jesus have hidden himself in the needs of Tutella Dhas to test the open doors of my heart—and to test the open doors of a church whose sign reads, "All are welcome here"?

Sadly, Tutella and others like him remain far removed from the intimate places of our lives and community experiences. It's Tutella that reminds me that community provides accountabilty. Tutella has to be included in community for his voice to be heard and our lives to be changed.

SEVERED MEMBERS

The apostle Paul reminds us that the church is the body of Christ. In our lack of solidarity and in our fractured communities, that body has become disjointed. It is a tragedy that secondary doctrinal issues have made us unable to embrace fellow Christians as brothers and sisters in Christ. Styles of worship, views on church leadership, varying perspectives on the use of spiritual gifts, and discussions on God's foreknowledge in relationship to humanity's free will often divide the body of Christ. When this happens, it is as if the body of Christ has severed its own members.

Trying to open a peanut shell is a difficult task for any three-year-old, but for Grace, who only has one arm, life provides even greater difficulties. As a three-month-old baby, Grace lost her father, sister and grandparents in an RUF rebel attack in Sierra Leone. Her left arm was hacked off with a machete. Watching her struggle to open a peanut, I was reminded of the struggle that it is for the dismembered body of Christ to respond to the needs of the world.

As a disjointed body, we find it difficult to perform the tasks that are expected of us. Look around the world today. The world is a place marked by suffering and poverty. Where is the church? In isolated instances, the body of Christ is able to respond effectively; however, most of those who need the embrace of the body of Christ never feel it. The image of little Grace and her amputated arm is as tragic as the reality of a divided church. But unlike the church, Grace didn't choose to sever her arm. Grace and the thousands of others like her need a stronger embrace from us, Christ's body.

SHARING A MEAL

When I used to live in India, my apartment was located at the end of a dirt road in a neighborhood known as "Majestic Colony."[16] Every time I needed to go somewhere or get something, I had to walk 150 yards down this road and turn left toward the markets and stores.

Halfway along the journey, the road became paved, but the area was still extremely poor. On both sides of the street were houses, shacks, slums and structures inhabited by families struggling to stay alive. There were piles of trash and waste swept to the side of the street. The area looked devastated, the way you'd imagine a street would look after a war.

It was a pretty cheerless and dismal street, a stark example of the urban residential poverty and disparity of India. If it weren't for the little children playing blissfully along the road, it could have been a very depressing sight.

One small child there, Devi, has since become a dear, lifelong friend. I would usually make a point to look for her if she didn't find me first. Devi had big, gorgeous brown eyes, long eyelashes, long stringy black hair and high cheekbones, and she was missing her left front tooth. She had to be the cutest kid on the block.

Devi's family was wonderful. She was the youngest of five daughters: Sujana was twenty, Maya was eighteen, Padma was sixteen, Rani was eleven, and Devi was eight. Both their parents worked very hard. Their father was a construction worker, and their mother made and sold long strings of tiny jasmine flowers that women wear in their hair.

Their home was a little, thatch-roofed shanty constructed in the seven feet between two old, dilapidated brick houses. It was where they ate, slept, cooked their food, did their homework, played their games and prayed before their statue of Ganesh (the elephant-headed god of prosperity).

They became a sort of family to me. Occasionally, I'd stop by in the evenings to share a cup of tea with their father, trying to fumble through his limited English and my even more limited Tamil. I would play jacks with the girls or look at the little book of family photos that they cherished among their most prized possessions. Their little home in the slums had been a refuge for me in many times of frustration.

There was one night that I'll never forget. It was dark. They did not have electricity in their home even when my power was on, so they depended on the streetlights for some of their light. They had two small candles burning, casting a dim, golden light on the dirty walls and dirt floor. They sat me down on the only stool in the place, and we tried to talk. A little Tamil here and a little English there, and we knew, more or less, that everyone was okay and doing well. Then the girls invited me to stay for dinner.

So many times I had walked by and they had asked, *"Saap teeng lah?"* ("Have you eaten?"), and just as many times they had invited me to join them for lunch or dinner. Every time I declined. It wasn't that I didn't want to eat with them. It was that I always felt they needed all the food they had, and sharing with me would only mean that they'd go without. This time, however, I felt that I needed to stay.

I tried to help Maya and Padma cook. There wasn't much that I could help with. They had a few worn-out, metal vessels to cook dinner in and an open fire in the corner. First, they cooked a big pot of plain rice, and then they started on the curry. Since I was there, they wanted to give me the best, so Rani ran to the store to get a few eggs.

There wasn't a lot of food, but it took an hour to prepare the meal. When it was ready, we sat cross-legged on the dirt floor and Maya served us. We each received a few spoons of plain rice and then a very small portion of egg curry to mix in with the rice. My heart broke as she served us. The girls hardly had anything for themselves, yet they were so happy to share with me. We sat together, barefoot, eating with our hands, happy and content. It was a priceless communion that satisfied my soul.

When everyone had eaten, we sat around and listened to some soft Tamil music on an old, beat-up transistor radio. It was perfect. The later it got, the more sleepy we all became, and soon it was time to lay the little girls down to sleep. I said good night and walked past the gate into "Majestic Colony," back to my home.

A deep sadness accompanied me home. That night I lay down on my own mattress on the floor and, with a candle burning beside me, said a prayer for my little friends—my friends who work harder than, but eat less than, anyone I know; my friends who give so much but get so very little; my friends who seem to have so much joy, despite their poverty; my friends who were sleeping on the ground and who were probably still hungry.

GOD'S GIFT TO THE WORLD
The Western church, for the most part living in a "Majestic Colony," has mistaken God's financial blessings as individual provision rather than resources with potential for kingdom development. With this misunderstanding has come an unwillingness to recognize and identify with Jesus' model of ministry and application of holiness. Our relationships with and perceptions of those under the cruelty of oppression will be the perfect testing ground to validate God's redemptive work of sanctification.

David Chronic, Europe and Africa regional coordinator for Word Made Flesh, helped our community find a trajectory for this years ago when he wrote,

> We are called to seek Jesus among the poorest of the poor. In heeding this call, we desire to offer ourselves to the poor. Our tendency, however, is to invite the poor into our community. We hope to build an open, honest, healing community into which the poor can be integrated. But the poor do not need to be integrated into our community. God is calling us, rather, to identify with theirs. When we move from integration to identification, we close the gap between having two communities: the helpers and the helped, the workers with the poor and the poor themselves.[17]

Mother Teresa repeatedly shared that we need the poor much more than they need us. She is right. God often uses people who are poor to induce social holiness. Through the example of our friends who suffer in poverty, we are humbled. Through the example of those who are weak, perceived as foolish and on the margins, we are instructed. Those on the margins have a lot to teach us, yet our pride often prevents us from learning from them.

The faith of the North American church has become very exclusive. If someone does not fit the social and economic mold of our churches, they may have a tough time being accepted by the Christians there. How many of us wouldn't stare if someone who prostitutes walked into the sanctuary on Sunday morning—would not wonder why he or she was there, would not judge and criticize him or her in our hearts and minds? Those who prostituted in first-century Palestine felt as if they could spend time with Jesus—why can't they feel the same way with his followers?

Jesus' ministry was not to the upper class, the educated, the elite or the most influential social figures. Jesus came and ministered among those who were poor, with the poor and as a poor man. His ministry was to the children, those who were begging, victims of leprosy, the woman at the well, the woman caught in the act of adultery, the tax collectors, the fishermen communities and those on the margins. Jesus came to the common people and lived alongside them. As a church, we must learn new ways to celebrate our faith inclusively so that those on the margins of society will feel welcome—and so that our love and acceptance of the other will aid in our paths to holiness.

Jesus' ministry was marked with a distinctive compassion for the oppressed poor. The first recorded words coming from the mouth of Jesus as he began his public ministry are found in Luke 4:18-19. Jesus entered the synagogue, unrolled the scrolls of Isaiah and read the fulfilled prophecy: "The Spirit of the Lord is upon me, because he has anointed me to preach good news to the poor. He has sent me to proclaim freedom for the prisoners and recovery of sight for the blind, to release the oppressed, to proclaim the year of the Lord's favor."

He was approached by the religious, the educated and even the rich. Who can forget his encounter with the rich young ruler: "Go sell everything you have and give it to the poor . . . then come and follow me" (Mark 10:21; see also Matthew 19:21). When John's disciples were sent to question if Jesus was the Christ, the response sent in return was "The good news is preached to the poor" (Matthew 11:5). In Luke, the Sermon on the Mount states in the Beatitudes, "Blessed are you who are poor, for yours is the kingdom of God" (Luke 6:20).

In the Gospel of Matthew, we find Jesus identifying himself with the afflictions and sufferings of the poor. In Matthew 25:42-43 we read the familiar passage, "For I was hungry and you gave me nothing to eat, I was thirsty and you gave me nothing to drink, I was a stranger and you did not invite me in, I needed clothes and you did not clothe me, I was sick and in prison and you did not look after me."

As we look upon the faces of our friends who are poor, as we see the children, friends begging on the streets, and those in need, we are being confronted by Christ. He is placing before us an opportunity to love and serve him through the needs of the impoverished. He is offering an invitation to his community.

The gospel clearly shows us the love and compassion that God has for the oppressed. From the beginning to the end, the Bible is full of references to those in need and on the margins.

- In the Hebrew Bible, the laws of Deuteronomy show a special concern for people who are poor—ultimately a call to radical community (see Deuteronomy 14:28-29; 15:7-11; 16:11-14, 18; 24:14-15, 17-21).

- The poetic literature of the Psalms portrays God as a defender of the defenseless and a father to the fatherless (see Psalms 10:14; 41:1; 68:5-6; 109:6-16; 132:15; 146:7).

- The wisdom of Proverbs defines a generous person as one who shares with those who are poor. Passages in Proverbs illustrate God's love for those who are poor (see Proverbs 14:31; 19:17; 21:13; 22:9; 28:5; 29:7; 31:8-9).

- The prophets close the Hebrew Bible with strong words of judgment on a nation that has turned its back on God and closed its ears to the cries of those who are poor (see Isaiah 1:17; 3:14-15; 11:1-5; 28:17; 58:5-10; Jeremiah 2:34; 5:27-28; 7:5-7; 22:3, 16; 49:11; Ezekiel 16:49; Hosea 2:19; 10:12; Amos 5:7, 10-15, 24; 8:4-6; Micah 2:1-3; 3:1-3, Habbakuk 1:3-4; Zechariah 7:10).

If we look through the rest of the New Testament, we continue to find references to our brothers and sisters in need. In the book of James, we find a letter full of references to our sisters and brothers in need and how we should conduct ourselves on their behalf. James reminds us of the life that we are called to live: "Religion that

God our Father accepts as pure and faultless is this: to look after orphans and widows in their distress and to keep oneself from being polluted by the world" (James 1:27).

FRACTURED COMMUNITY AND POVERTY

I would have to say that it is my friends who are poor who have taught me the most about community. Now I know that friendship and community are not the same thing. My friends in the red-light districts, on the streets, and living in slums and favelas and refugee camps have invited me into an expression of community marked by grace and love unlike any other I've experienced.

The Scriptures have plenty to say about our global neighbors who are poor, but what is poverty? What are the issues involved? How is community central in this conversation?

On one level, the church has isolated itself from those who are poor. It can be said that we worship in a sound-proof, glass sanctuary. As the statistics of poverty grow, the church only sings louder so as not to hear the staggering numbers and the cries of the victims.

I believe that God is using the cries of our friends who suffer in poverty today to call the church out of its sound-proof sanctuaries. God is challenging the church to respond to a world in need. Too often, however, the church has isolated itself and failed to listen, and thus contributed to the suffering. God is calling us to establish communities that offer the prophetic presence of Christ in today's world.

In the isolation of those who are poor and the insulation from the oppressed, the individual members of the church have caused a deep fragmentation and division within the corporate members of the church. This fractured fragmentation and division of community poses a problem in light of an impoverished world. Because of isolation and insulation, the lack of community offered to those in our global family who are poor is yet another cause of marginalization and, in turn, a cause of poverty.

On another level, the church often isolates the poor. I have walked out of countless churches almost everywhere I've traveled, only to be greeted by a long line of people who are begging at the gate of the building. These men and women know "their place"— they stand outside the gates. Do our multi-million-dollar sanctuaries in North America send the same message?

There is a popular misconception that financial blessing is an indication of right standing before God. This leads to the judgment that people who are poor are thus outside of right relationship with God. The assumption is made that when poor people are saved, their financial problems will be cured. Those who hold to this belief, despite its obvious flaws, isolate people who are poor by placing unfounded judgment on their spirituality by observing their physical conditions. This lie, that poverty is a judgment of God as a result of broken relationship with God, strips away compassion and denies our friends who are poor God's love and mercy.

I've visited enough fishing villages in South India to find one consistent reality. Among a predominantly Hindu village there will be perhaps a hundred Muslims with one mosque, and there will be forty Christians with five churches. These churches will represent the various denominations of the region; all members of one body, yet they have very little tolerance for one another.

While Christianity is fractured, the Muslims, who are famous for brotherhood, take the appealing edge. Poor people know their need for community. They affirm their need for one another. They find strength in numbers. How can the church expect those on the margins to join it if the church can't offer them the one thing that they know they need?

These first issues, isolation and fractured community, both communicate themselves in terms of a broken relationship between those who are poor and the church. Until this relationship is healed and we initiate reconciliation between God and humanity, there can be no authentic kingdom community.

In too many instances, the church has been tight-fisted and stingy. It is so tempting to simply make more and give less. Mother Teresa said, "If the poor die of hunger, it is not because God does not care for them. Rather, it is because neither you nor I are generous enough."[18]

In a world where the chasm between the rich and the poor continually widens, it is critical that we in the church reach out in willingness to share the financial blessings God has graciously poured upon us. According to United Nations Development Program figures, "The richest 20 percent of the world's population receives 82.7 percent of the total world income while the poorest 20 percent receives only 1.4 percent. Global economic growth rarely filters down."[19]

In the context of a dying world, the church must redefine spirituality and seek a new understanding of holiness as it relates to justice. Part of that re-defining process must involve a reversal in our understanding of possessions. If the church continues to hold tightly to its material wealth, those in real and desperate need will continue to go without. Selfishness only contributes to the global disparity that excludes those who are poor, and in part defines as well as perpetuates poverty.

One prevalent belief that hinders authentic community is the assumption that poor people cannot help themselves. Oftentimes the church develops projects and programs that impose themselves upon those who are poor, further distancing any relationship with those we desperately need to consider friends. In defining poverty, a portion of that definition should include poverty as "the inability to change circumstances," *not* the inability to help oneself.

The church regularly approaches mission as a means of assuming leadership positions over the target group or region. Unfortunately, the stereotypes of the imperialistic missionary and the culturally insensitive Christian worker are all too true. The church's history in missions work has been commonly marked by insensitivity and inappropriateness.

Unless our communities among friends who are poor are founded in personal humility, there can be no fruit. We must minister among and with the broken out of a posture of brokenness; it is the only way we will be accepted. When we realize that we have as much to learn as we have to offer, true Christlike ministry will freely flow, community will develop, and we will be transformed.

Jayakumar Christian says, "When we invest our money in the poor, we make the poor into beggars; when we invest in programs for the poor, we turn the poor into beneficiaries; when we invest our life in the poor, the poor will reap life."[20]

"We are all called to minister to the poor," writes Viv Grigg in the book *Companion to the Poor*. "Such a ministry is the logical obedience of any disciple imitating the attitudes, character, and teaching of Jesus. He commands everyone to renounce all (Luke 14:33), to give to the poor and live simply."[21]

The point is not only that Jesus focused on those who were poor, but that he came and lived among them. In the story where Jesus healed the man possessed by the legion of demons, the account in Matthew states, "He arrived at the *other side*" (Matthew 8:28). Jesus got into the boat and went. The mission is that simple. It is a call to go, to make disciples, to baptize and to teach (see Matthew 28:18-19).

Has the church forgotten its mission? Has the church, in an ever-present quest for ease and convenience, altered the final command of our Master? Unless the original mission of our Master is remembered, then our friends who are poor will go without a partner, without a servant, and without a community. In such a case, there will be no kingdom community. Thus, our friends who are poor will remain in need due to the disobedience of the church.

GIVING OUR LEFTOVERS

As a senior at Asbury College in Wilmore, Kentucky, I was beginning to develop consciousness and compassion for those who were poor. One evening before Christmas as I walked into the cafeteria, I saw a sign for "Toys for Tots," a program that makes opportunities available for those in a community to give gifts to poor and needy people in the community. I went up to the table to do my duty and buy a little boy a football for Christmas.

I asked the student volunteer seated at the table for a small boy's Christmas wish list. I just wanted to buy some little kid a football.

The man informed me that all the children were taken care of; it was their parents that no one wanted to buy gifts for. I gladly accepted the wish list of a man in the community, a father of three. The only thing this man asked for was a pair of pants, size 32. A pair of pants was all that he wanted, and he couldn't afford it himself. I thought, *I can have a friend drive me to Wal-Mart so that I can find this man a $14 pair of pants.*

That evening I sat on my couch and picked up the J. Crew catalogue (nothing like old school J. Crew). I also needed a pair of pants that Christmas and was about to order myself a $44 pair of khaki chinos when I remembered the man's wish list.

That's when God convicted me. I was suddenly reminded that when I give to those who are poor, I am giving to Jesus (see Proverbs 19:17). This father of three was offering me an opportunity to serve Jesus, to buy Jesus a pair of pants for Christmas. And there I was, ready to buy "Jesus" a pair of pants at Wal-Mart and then order myself a pair of pants that cost three times as much!

As soon as I realized what I was doing, I was broken. I decided to buy this man the nicest pants I could afford. I opened the opportunity up to my friends and invited them to pitch in if they were willing. As I presented this request, they all responded in the same way: "Hey, I have a pair of pants that size that I never wear anymore. Should we give him these?"

I began to see how we give to those who are poor. We figure people who are poor don't mind what we give them, that they'll take anything. So we give them our leftovers.

What if Jesus came to the door right now? What would he say? "I'm in town for a few days, do you know where I might be able to find a cheap hotel?" Immediately I would offer Jesus my own bed, insisting that he take it. He then might ask, "I'm hungry. Where might I be able to get a loaf of bread or a can of soup?" Of course, I would sit the Master down at my own dining table and prepare a feast for him.

That's how I would treat Jesus. But how do I treat my friends who are poor? How do I look my neighbors in the eye and recognize the sufferings of Christ in their poverty?

The teacher of the law confronted Jesus with this very question in Luke 10:25-28. The expert asked Jesus how to obtain eternal life. Jesus tested this man and asked him what he thought the law said. The expert replied, "'Love the Lord your God with all your heart and with all your soul and with all your strength and with all your mind'; and 'Love your neighbor as yourself.'" Jesus responded, "You have answered correctly. Do this and live." Our love for God is seen in our love for our neighbor.

Do we see the child in need, begging on the streets, and automatically want the best education, clothes, food, and housing for that child? Do we see our own children and want the best for them? Do we love the child who begs as we love ourselves and as we love our own children? How can we love God and not love God's children? Those who are poor are "God's people" (Isaiah 3:15), but do we treat them like that? Or do we show a love that is based in partiality?

Until the church learns to love its neighbor as itself, a lack of love and compassion will allow the church to neglect the needs of our sisters, brothers and global neighbors who go without. Will the church remain isolated from Devi? Will the church continue to be a broken community that Devi will want no part of? Will the church continue to hold its resources so tightly that the very things Devi needs for basic daily survival won't be given to her? Will the church offer Devi an imperialistic program with unrealistic demands and handouts only to degrade her and string her out? Will the church ever go to Devi? Will the church love Devi, even though this poor little girl is dirty and sleeps on a mud floor?

The church has the answer, if only we will leave our "majestic colony" and follow the example of Christ who enters into community with those who are poor and offers a hand to alleviate the suffering of Devi and others.

Community is a tangible sign of the kingdom. When communities marked by submission and sacrifice are developed, the fruits naturally follow, often effortlessly. Henri Nouwen writes, "Wherever true Christian community is formed, compassion *happens* in the world."²² Compassion happens as an act because in community, suffering with others tests the cords that bind communities together. If a community is unable to suffer together, it is unable to suffer with those who are poor. Therefore, by its mere nature, community produces compassion.

The strength of a community that bears the fruit of compassion can be seen in its ability to receive others in its midst. I have often been included in different communities that have failed miserably in this area. It has been those communities that continue to grow by adding and receiving new members, sometimes very different and unique members, which keep the life of the community fresh and vibrant. When a community becomes closed or exclusive, the death of that community is imminent. Further, it is when communities are able to absorb people who are poor among them that maturity sets in. Jean Vanier writes, "An openness to the weak and the needy in our own groups help us to open our hearts to others who are weak and needy in the greater group of humanity. It is the first sign of a healthy group. A healthy bonding leads us to a greater love for others."[23]

When our friends who are poor are central in our communities, it keeps our hearts open and available to a compassionate response to the needs of the world. This response comes from affirming it as our own response of God's love to the condition of our heart, allowing that to be transferred through us to the condition of the world. In community, this transfer includes these needs as a sign of Jesus among us.

The great Indian mystic Sadhu Sundar Singh said, "The great gift of service is that it also helps the one who serves."[24] He went on to wrap community around these words. He told of a journey in Tibet where the temperature suddenly dropped and he feared for his life. As he went on, he stumbled over a body covered in snow and barely alive. Sadhu Sundar Singh told his guide they would carry this man to the next village to help save his life. The guide refused, fearful for his own life; he left the freezing man and the sadhu behind.

After a long and treacherous journey, night began to fall and the sadhu finally came upon a village only to discover the frozen and dead body of his guide. The sadhu's companion had died within shouting distance of the village.

It was the weight of the man that the sadhu had carried which had created enough body heat to keep both him and the victim warm enough to survive the journey. They both made it safely to the village because they had one another. The sadhu commented, "No on can live without the help of others, and in helping others, we receive help ourselves."[25]

It's the weight of community, the joys and sorrows, that saves us. This burden has saved me.

3. SIMPLICITY

Several years back, Phileena and I spent six months living in Lima, Peru, with the Word Made Flesh staff there. Our last day, July 28, 2000, was Peru's Independence Day and happened to be the inauguration of the then re-elected president, Alberto Fujimori.

Many political historians considered Fujimori a dictator. Prior to the 2000 elections, he had changed the Peruvian constitution to allow himself to run for an unprecedented third presidential term. When the Peruvian Supreme Court protested, he dismissed four of the seven judges. When it looked as if the lead opposition candidate, Alejandro Toledo, was going to win the elections, a "miraculous" surge of votes for Fujimori—over one million more votes cast than registered voters—forced a run-off election in May.

In the second round of elections held on May 28, 2000, the Peruvian government rejected offers from neutral international monitoring organizations to oversee the voting process that had been accused of electoral fraud. Toledo boycotted the runoff elections, so Fujimori ran formally unopposed. Demonstrations and protests throughout the country followed the announcement of his victory and third presidential term.

Toledo called for four days of nonviolent, peaceful marches during the week of Independence Day. They were to culminate at the presidential palace to prevent Fujimori from being inaugurated.

On Friday, July 28, the gagged media was silent as Fujimori turned 40,000 police against an unarmed civilian population.

The demonstrations and marches were intended to be peaceful. To justify police repression against the people, Vladimiro Montesinos—enigmatic head of the Peruvian intelligence agency and an internationally wanted spy and criminal—reportedly sent over a hundred infiltrators into the crowds to stir up violence and unrest. As Fujimori was being sworn in, Associate Press journalist Rich Vecchio wrote, "The battle raged from one street corner to the next, the tear gas canisters tracing an arcing plume of smoke across an overcast sky before dropping into the crowds."[1]

That afternoon I was in the middle of the battle zone with Walter Forcatto, one of my closest friends and, at the time, Word Made Flesh Peru field director. At one point, we were even marching with Toledo, close enough to put a hand on his shoulder, when the black-clad riot troopers started shooting tear gas at us. The noxious gas burned our eyes as we ran coughing and choking; on numerous occasions throughout the day, we found ourselves doubled-over, gagging as the tear gas scorched our throats and blinded our eyes. A week later, the skin on our faces was peeling like sunburn because of all the tear gas we had been exposed to throughout that day.

It had been a day of warring. More than two hundred civilians had been wounded by stray bullets or shot with flaming tear gas canisters. Countless others had been arrested or were missing. Witnessing the spilled blood of the oppressed at the hands of an unjust structure, I prayed in my heart and on my lips for revolution—revolution and freedom for the oppressed poor people of Peru.

PREOCCUPATION

I traveled directly from Lima's battle zone to the quiet and tranquil small town of Wilmore, Kentucky, where I was greeted by soft Kentucky summer rain and the chimes of the Asbury College bell tower. From one seemingly incongruous context to the other in less than twenty-four hours. With an estimated more than 80,000 demonstrators marching in the streets of Lima, a city under a cloud of tear gas and streets stained with the blood of peaceful protesters, much of the world sat by unaware and unconcerned.

Many of us think that our personal geographical context justifies our disengagement from the hurt and pain of the rest of the world. We presume that if there were oppressed or starving members in our local churches, we would alter our spending and giving habits enough to keep them from starving to death. But those who go without the basic necessities of life, regardless of their geographical location or proximity, are nevertheless counted as part of our family: fellow believers in the Sudan or Sri Lanka or Peru are as much an intrinsic part of the body of Christ as are the Methodists, Presbyterians, or Catholics down the street. Even more, though many of those trapped in oppressive and unjust poverty around the world are theologically our brothers and sisters, all are our neighbors. Their misery is our misery, their suffering is—or should be—our suffering.

An unarguable Christian response to this reality is summed up well in a familiar challenge often ascribed to Gandhi: "Live simply that others may simply live."

Simplicity is a hard one for me. I try to hide the struggle by masking certain things in my life as certifiably simple, but there are plenty of illustrations that would challenge this.

Though I'm not a homeowner, I believe in book ownership. I have a library full of them. The inevitable first question someone poses on their initial visit to my library is, "Have you read *all* these books?" I fumble for a tidy way to avoid answering the question with the direct answer, "No," by saying goofy things like "I've read *in* most of them," or "Some of these are for reference." But the truth is, I often wonder what the thousands of books on my shelves say about my personal view of simplicity. And that's only one example of many that I could share.

Christians have done a lot to complicate simplicity. Our internal angst regarding the issue has spun itself off into complex formulas and a myriad of books to help us simplify our lives. Ironically, I've actually spent quite a bit of money on books about simplicity and, rightly so, feel further from understanding it after having read them. And I always feel cheated after reading them. Not sure why, but I always expect (maybe hope) that the next book or article on simplicity will offer the magic formula for success. Somehow I think someone will finally be able to wrap a definition around the concept and give me the keys to make it work in my own life. I'm still waiting.

A few years ago, I bought Phileena a subscription to the magazine *Real Simple*. We thought it could be a fresh take on the subject with practical ideas to help our journey. Wow. Who knew we'd have to completely redecorate our home to be "real simple." Too bad it costs so much to simplify.

Simplicity is hard. Far from simple. And it's hard to keep it simple when our cultural context insulates and isolates us from the rest of the world. It's easy to see the gross abuse of power in the corruption of Fujimori. It's a little harder but still easy enough to see a Kentucky small-town community like the one I lived in fall into the trappings of excess and intemperance without the prophetic presence of the poor in our lives. The complexities and corresponding demands on life have often clouded my vision of my reality, a reality that is intrinsically connected to the circumstances of my global neighbors. I find myself falling into a life that rejects simplicity by complicating the very faith that Christ made simple.

THE PROPHETIC PRESENCE OF THOSE WHO ARE POOR

Moving to the edge of a slum in Chennai, I was young and ambitious. I was fresh out of college with my shiny new degree in theology, missiology and biblical languages. Poverty surrounded me and helped redefine what I thought I "needed." My flat was meager and hardly furnished. I had a mattress on the floor in my bedroom, a couple wicker chairs in the living room, a few surfing posters and a picture of Bob Marley on the wall, a small library, and the equivalent of a camping stove that I screwed on top of a replaceable gas canister.

Really, compared to most people I'd known in my life, I thought I was living simply. That was, until my neighbors would come to visit. All these kids from the slums found out where I lived and would make their way over to my flat just to stand at the door looking in. Sometimes they'd come in, and we'd sit in the chairs and try to figure out what one another was saying (my Tamil wasn't so good).[2] They always wanted to check the place out and would walk from the living room into the kitchen or the bedroom. I often noticed them turning the faucets on or gazing at lights I had forgotten to turn off when leaving a room.

They didn't have to say anything to remind me that they didn't have ceiling fans at their homes or running water. They didn't have electricity either, and wasting mine wasn't winning me any popularity points in their eyes. I knew my waste was offensive to them.

These children's presence in my home was always convicting. Simplicity quickly became a commitment to living a lifestyle that reflected respect for their circumstances, for their poverty. My poor friends became a prophetic presence of grace that challenged my assumptions on how entitled I felt to hold onto God's expression of provision in my life. The proverb "I cried because I had no shoes until I saw the man who had no feet" took on new meaning.

Though I don't live on the edge of a slum anymore, discovering and learning to celebrate simplicity continues to be a hallmark of grace in my life. Practically, simplicity has become my posture and intention to live free from the bondage and control of anything other than the embrace of God. Essentially, simplicity is letting God truly be God, surrendering to that in all areas of life as an act of submission to God and humanity. The prophetic presence of the poor in my life has also made simplicity one of the rare things that is easier done than said. I mean, how do I talk about it? What can be said? The more I try to find language for it, the more confusing it seems to get. Why is simplicity so complex?

Keeping it simple always seems to be so complicated for me.

JESUS' MODEL OF SIMPLICITY

Did Jesus embrace simplicity? On one hand, we learn that Jesus had "no place to lay his head" (Matthew 8:20; Luke 9:58). In an age when many Western Christians are homeowners, it's hard to imagine that our Savior was, in a sense, homeless. We also learn that Jesus and the disciples were supported by a group of generous women (Luke 8:3). Technically, it seems Jesus was unemployed. Jesus even needed to borrow a ride into Jerusalem during the week of his passion. No home, no job, and no wheels. Simple? Or poor?

On the other hand, New Testament scholar Joel Green points out that "Jesus' dependence on the benefaction of others (Luke 8:3) has already ruled out any picture in Luke of an ascetic Jesus who rejects outright the use of wealth."[3] Further, it seems more often than not, Jesus' meetings took place at feasts. In his parables, he spoke of banquets and promised great feasts to the faithful. The first recorded miracle of Christ was turning water into wine (John 2:1-12.); in fact, because wine was often part of his interactions, some thought Jesus had an alcohol problem (Matthew 11:19; Luke 7:34). We see Mary accepting gifts of great value at the birth of Jesus (Matthew 2:11), and Jesus himself not only allowed a woman to pour expensive perfume over him but scolded his disciples for their audacious remarks about how that could have been sold and the proceeds given to people who were poor. After the crucifixion, we're told Jesus was laid in the tomb of a rich man and given the works, including seventy-five pounds of myrrh (not cheap back in the day) with which to embalm his corpse (John 19:38-41).

So we have this homeless, unemployed man without a ride, going out drinking with friends, always talking about great feasts and banquets, and accepting gifts of tremendous value—even having perfume poured over his feet, and then sparing no expense for his burial. It can be confusing. Are these things contrary to simplicity? Does the life of Christ support or oppose austerity? How can we make sense of this?

I find a direct correlation between simplicity and the table. There's something existential and mystical that happens to me around the table. There's something about a shared meal that provokes my internal yearnings for the eternal—for the table at the great banquet in paradise, the table Christ always spoke of. Christine Pohl hints at this in her book on the historical Christian discipline of hospitality when she writes, "In the context of shared meals, the presence of God's Kingdom is prefigured, revealed, and reflected."[4] To me, that's almost sacramental.

In my experience, the table is a place where we are disarmed. The table allows both rich and poor to find their place in the human family, a family that, according to the apostle Paul, needs to strive toward an equality of justice. In 2 Corinthians 8:14, he writes, "Your plenty will supply what they need, so that in turn their plenty will supply what you need." The goal is equality.

This can only happen when a community takes it upon itself to celebrate simplicity as a collective commitment to justice. In Sandra Wheeler's book on wealth and possessions, she puts it this way: "Therefore the community formed by that grace is one marked by openheartedness and equity, in which gifts are given without mixed motives, resources are shared, and the needs of all are met—and its norm is equality."[5]

SIMPLICITY AT THE TABLE

Now I'm not a big fan of short-term missions. I myself have made several short-term trips, and I can certainly attest to the impact they have made on me personally. However, it seems like we are living in a day where short-term missions have become a form of Christian tourism or spiritual adventurism. In most cases, it's honestly embarrassing for me to bring a group of loud Americans (yes, sometimes I have been known to be the loudest) into the poorest parts of the Majority World—for all the obvious reasons. At the same time, making introductions for the non-poor with our friends on the margins can create tremendous opportunities for personal formation and corporate transformation.

Anyway, I used to bring a lot of groups to India. We would usually budget $5.00 per person per meal for food. During their visit, I would intentionally bring them to my favorite little local places and strongly encourage them not to waste food—even if that meant ordering only what we could actually eat rather than what we thought we wanted to try. I would constantly remind them that it was our luxury to sit down over a hot meal and that we needed to practice sincere gratitude as we remembered those going without. We would also often invite local friends (many of them extremely poor) to join us, their presence a constant reminder not to waste.

At the end of these trips, I would total up the food costs for the group. On every trip, there was good news to report. On average, even after picking up the tab for all our friends and guests, we would end up spending around $2.00-2.50 per person per meal, finding ourselves with a surplus of unused budgeted lunch money.

We saved a lot of money that way. Now sure, saving $2.50 at a meal or two doesn't really add up to a whole lot. But with 12 people saving $2.50 a meal for two weeks, we suddenly found over twelve hundred dollars that we had to share.

The conversations were lively. In a place like India, $1,200 has the potential to go a long way. This particular group discussed how we could find ways to allow our simplicity at the table to help feed those who didn't have adequate nutrition and were suffering from hunger.

Food expenses were always my favorite to manipulate in this way because, as Christine Pohl writes, "The practice of hospitality almost always includes eating meals together. Sustained hospitality requires a light hold on material possessions and a commitment to a simplified life-style."[6] The reminder of our friends, and, in many cases, their actual presence at the table, introduced an expression of simplicity that was honoring and redemptive. Redemptive because by remembering friends who are poor each time we sat at a table, we ordered what we needed, not what we wanted.

In India there is also the very real, and understandable, pressure to feel guilty about sitting down at the table. Wheeler again writes, "Possessions become useful and acceptable within the Christian community exactly insofar as they become dispensable to their possessors, and thus available for dispersal as the material needs of others, or the spiritual needs of their erstwhile owners, make it expedient."[7] Moving from guilt to generosity always makes a big impact on people's worldviews.

These were always simple experiments in personal economics. Somehow it was always easier to work this out on a personal level than a structural one. Too easily and too often, we spiritualize Western forms of capitalism and demonize socialism to justify over-consumption and unresponsiveness to the global demands of justice and equality. We theologize material provision as "God's blessing" while failing to recognize that perhaps the material provision placed in our trust may, in fact, be intended to advance God's kingdom or benefit someone else, like the women who funded Jesus' ministry or the man who provided Jesus' tomb.

I believe that simplicity was not only lived and taught by Jesus but is demanded of his followers. The table is a safe place to start practicing this.

However, for simplicity to be authentic in our lives, it has to revolutionize our hearts. There is nothing we have done in the so-called Developed World to earn our fortunate position, and God does not owe us any favors. The "accident" of where we were born may, in fact, be part of the complexity of working out our salvation with fear and trembling—being born in the prosperous West may demand that we more intently practice generosity than those "accidentally" born into hardship in Africa, Asia, or South America. The "accident" of being born in North America may be the eye of the needle that we have tried so hard to push our camels through.

We all know this. Opportunity and privilege carry with them great responsibility. We have all been exposed to the images and news of the world's suffering, and that exposure demands a response. So I pray for revolution—a revolution that would make all of us free so that none would be oppressed. I believe simplicity is this revolution.

SCARCITY AND ABUNDANCE

I often feel conflicted regarding how to live. Sometimes I look at my hands, palms open facing upward, and think of the dead bodies I've carried or the children I've buried because of AIDS in South India. Sometimes, when gathered around the table with friends, I hold up a glass of wine to toast, only to stare at the cup while recalling the empty plates and bare tables of my friends all around the world—friends going to bed hungry again while I celebrate and feast. Trying to make sense of the disparity is one of the most painful and difficult challenges of my life.

And yet one of the greatest gifts given to us by our friends who are poor is the ability to celebrate.

Some of the best, and wildest, parties I've ever been to have been thrown by some of the poorest people I know. They spare no expense. People who literally don't have the money to send their kids to school have served me the best meals or bought the most extravagant gifts for me over the years. The generosity of friends who are poor confounds me, and it is consistent around the world. Why is that? Why do people who are poor seem to know how to celebrate better than anyone else? Is it because the vacillation between joy and sorrow is so real in their lives that they have an ability to go deeper in joy due to the depths of their sorrows?

The Lebanese poet and mystic Khalil Gibran writes about this in the literary classic *The Prophet*. In what might be his most riveting and beautiful work, he says, "Joy is your sorrow unmasked. The deeper that sorrow carves into your being, the more joy you can contain."[8]

There's something about the sorrow of poverty that creates a tremendous capacity for joy in the souls of those who suffer the most.

On my first trip to India I learned this in the slums of Goa. A little girl taught me how to pray simple prayers. We would sit on the floor in her little home with her parents and two sisters. Her mother would bring out steaming heaps of plain white rice and serve it to us on banana leaves. Then she would pour a little dhal over the rice—not much, but just enough. From her experience of hunger, my friend Ezabella would pray with sincerity and gratefulness, "Lord, we thank you for providing this meal for us and pray that you would be with our friends who don't have a hot meal before them this evening." Opening my eyes after her simple prayer always transformed the meal. I found myself truly thankful for what seemed hardly appetizing before her prayer. Her prayers convicted me of my mentality of scarcity which caused me to look at the pile of rice as a feeble attempt to masquerade itself as a meal. Ezabella's mentality of abundance looked at the pile of rice before her as a feast—a true gift from God.

She and her family had nothing, yet they celebrated a meal of thanksgiving each time they sat on the floor of their slum and ate together.

Teetering between this mentality of scarcity and abundance is tricky. The poorest people I know are among the most generous, while many of the richest people I know seem to be stingy in comparison. I guess that makes sense. To attain even moderate security or meager affluence means you'd probably have to hold onto a lot of it along the way.

HOW YOU HOLD, NOT WHAT YOU HOLD

Simplicity is best understood in evaluating *how* we hold things, not just *what* we do or don't hold. For me, this lesson was a hard one to learn. In fact, I didn't truly understand it until I refused to give the equivalent of a dime to a little boy at the Victoria Monument in Kolkata, India.

I had decided to show our visiting friends some of Kolkata's history.[9] Monsoon season had brought heavy rain that summer day, but between showers we saw the Victoria Monument, one of the starkest reminders of the British Raj and English rule in India. Typical of the streets of Kolkata, people were everywhere.

As we left the monument, a small boy—no older than nine or ten—followed our group. He retained the untarnished look of innocence amid the cruelty and hostility of Kolkata, his big, dark eyes looking up at us as we walked, his tattered red shorts and dirty yellow T-shirt speaking of a hard life on the streets. He wore no shoes, his hair was tousled, and his skin was darker than that of most Bengalis. He went from one person to the next, telling us, in broken English, his sad story and asking for a couple of rupees.

His mother and father had died, he said, and he was very hungry. We weren't sure whether to believe him or not. He was one of thousands of children begging in India. The little boy followed us for what seemed like a mile. A few in our group struck up a conversation with him, but for the most part, we ignored him.

Regularly seeing far more people begging in Kolkata than we had money to help, we had the arguments for giving and not giving constantly tearing through our minds. On one hand, we assumed that giving to someone begging encourages a lifestyle of pathetic dependency. They all seem to have the same needs, but many of them fabricate stories to prey on the emotions of rich foreigners. It is also a challenge to determine whether the man, woman or child is being forced to beg. Black markets (informal economic endeavors) around the world have been known to kidnap children and intentionally mutilate them, gouge out their eyes, or otherwise maim them, then place them in strategic locations to earn money for their handlers. On the other hand, the man, woman, or child begging from you may literally be dying before your eyes. How, then, can you not give?

Scripture says, "Give to the one who asks you" (Matthew 5:42). But does that mean giving exactly *what* they ask? E. Stanley Jones suggests, "It doesn't say give to him what he asks. . . . It may be what he asks, or it may be something better than he asks."[10] What about our attitude and motivation for giving? Are we performing an act of kindness to get that person begging to leave us alone? Can we give only a handful of change and feel good about it? What if we don't give anything? The Scriptures also say, "I was hungry and you gave me nothing to eat" (Matthew 25:42). If we don't give, will God punish us?

Later that afternoon, one of our friends revealed that the little boy in the red shorts had sexually propositioned him. We listened in disbelief and horror. He had asked for a couple of rupees—not even a dime in U.S. currency—for something to eat, and we had walked on by. That night, we wondered in what dark room that child would be sexually abused so he could earn enough money to buy the food—money we had refused to give him.

Two rupees, that's all this little kid in Kolkata wanted, and I didn't give them to him. I thought those rupees were mine. I had yet to lay them down, to give them to the Lord. It is so embarrassing to tell this story, but that is usually how things in my life are. It's the small stuff; it's the little things that keep me from full obedience. Had I given my all to God, then "my" finances would have been God's to give through me to that child.

Maybe in holding what wasn't mine, I might have actually stolen from that boy. Isaiah 3:14-15 reads, "The plunder of the poor is in your houses. What do you mean by crushing my people and grinding the faces of the poor?" There are undoubtedly numerous ways to interpret the phrase "the plunder of the poor."

When forced to examine my attitudes toward giving, I often think of John Wesley.

One afternoon Wesley had gone to town to buy some pictures for his room. After hanging the images around his house, he heard a knock at the door. It was bitterly cold outside, and the wind was blowing. There stood a young woman and her obviously undernourished baby in arm, both poorly clothed. They were going from door to door, begging for food and money to provide them with warmer clothing.

Wesley put his hand in his pocket and pulled out what little change was left over from his day of shopping. He handed it over and sent the woman on her way. When he closed the door behind him and turned around, the pictures on his walls faced him as judges—the money he had spent on those very frames could have helped the young mother.

The plunder of the poor was in John Wesley's house—in fact, it was hanging on his walls, condemning him. He fell to his knees and made a pledge to God: he promised that if God would provide for his basic needs, then he would give everything beyond that to those in poverty. Wesley determined that to live a sufficiently austere lifestyle, he would need twenty-eight British pounds per year. The first year he earned thirty pounds, living on twenty-eight and giving the surplus to the poor. The second year he earned nearly sixty, the third year almost 100, and by the end of his life John Wesley was earning over fourteen hundred British pounds a year—living off of twenty-eight and giving the rest to help meet the needs of people who were poor.

He is famous for saying, "[When I die] if I leave behind me 10 pounds . . . you and all [humanity] may bear witness against me, that I have lived and died a thief and a robber."[11] Wesley made sure he never stole from the poor.

Possessions, insofar as they possess us, oppose the kingdom. Five times in John 10:11-18 Jesus tells us that he lays down what is perhaps, in economic terms, a person's ultimate possession—his life—for us. "No one takes it from me, but I lay it down of my own accord" (John 10:18). David Chronic regularly reminds us of this passage as it relates to his giving to people begging in Romania, where he currently lives. He gives to keep his heart soft and tender—to remind himself that those in need are not asking him for money, they're asking God to help them through David's responsiveness. He always reminds us that what they are asking for doesn't belong to him, and that is why he needs to remember to constantly be letting go of it.

Vocationally, I have given my life to serving those who are poor, but that afternoon at the Victoria Monument I couldn't cough up a couple rupees when a hungry child asked me for money. We want to make the issue about what we *give*, but in truth the issue is about what we keep.

NOT WHAT YOU GIVE BUT WHAT YOU KEEP

Deepa is twelve years old. I can't even begin to imagine the life she and her sister have been forced to endure. Today, she is orphaned. Her entire immediate family has died from AIDS.

When she was younger, Deepa's mother died from AIDS. A couple years ago when Phileena and I were in India visiting Deepa, her little sister, Charu, was still alive but very sick and dying from AIDS herself. We found out on that trip to the Word Made Flesh children's homes in Chennai that at that time Deepa's father was also dying from AIDS.

It was a hot South Indian summer afternoon. Deepa and Charu's father came to visit his daughters. He looked terrible. In the weeks leading up to the visit, his health had gotten progressively worse. He would frequently be found passed out in the communal toilet in his slum—sometimes lying in his own diarrhea. The man was obviously in the final stages of the disease. I thought his two little girls were going to splinter his frail bones when they jumped up onto his lap that afternoon.

A couple days after his visit, I got a call. Deepa's father had committed suicide. The humiliation, the pain and the decay of his body pushed him over the edge. He took his life to bring an end to his suffering.

As you can imagine, his daughters were heartbroken. Phileena and I rushed to the home to find Deepa and Charu weeping. We held these little ones close, prayed with them, tried to encourage them with Scripture and promised we'd be there for them when they needed us. Our hearts were broken.

In the sad series of goodbyes that our lives seem to offer us, it came time for Phileena and me to once again pack up and leave Chennai. We spent our last day with the children at the home.

Deepa and Charu stayed close to us the entire day. When everyone had hugged and exchanged goodbyes, tears streamed down all of our faces. We walked past the gates of the home, turned around one last time to wave, and noticed Deepa had run inside. Before we could close the gate, she came running out of the home with a single yellow rose bud in hand.

We couldn't hold back the tears. After her father had died, they cleaned out his slum and discovered that his only possession was a dismal potted rose bush with a solitary bud. Deepa stood there, her face soaked in her own tears, holding out the flower to Phileena. How could we take it? It was her inheritance, the last reminder of her deceased parents.

Today, I take that flower with me everywhere, showing it as often as I can to illustrate this little, tender, revolutionary heart. It is pressed into the place in my Bible where Jesus is in the temple spying on the donors to the treasury.

In the story, he calls his disciples over and lets them in on the scene that's unfolding. There are some wealthy folks making substantial offerings, when out of nowhere comes a poor widow. She puts some change in the collection, probably some near-valueless reworked Hasmonean copper coins. These guys are eager to figure out what Jesus has in mind, but what he tells them must have shocked them. Christ does not venerate the high rollers in the group but points out the widow and claims her as his own. "She's mine," he must have thought. "I choose her." He goes on to say, "All of these people gave their gifts out of their wealth; but she out of her poverty *put in all* she had to live on" (Luke 21:4). The story suddenly became not about what was given, but what was left over—*nothing*.

Deepa gave all she had—she held nothing back. Her gift to us is among our most treasured belongings to this day.

Deepa's is a completely different context, but it's our same world. She's part of a completely different family, but she's our sister as well. How do we follow Deepa to God's heart? Where do we find the courage to let a little orphaned girl's tragedy compel us to name the complexities in our faith that keep us from generosity and obedience?

Deepa helps me understand that simplicity and poverty, although cousins perhaps, aren't the same thing. Poverty is often chosen *for* someone; simplicity has to be chosen *by* someone. But when we follow the redemptive example of Christ, who, "though he was rich, . . . for your sake he became poor, so that you through his poverty might become rich" (2 Corinthians 8:9), we start to sense our own eyes being opened. Richard Foster puts it this way: "Poverty is a means of grace; simplicity is the grace itself."[12]

LOOSENING OUR GRASP

I travel frequently to speak at colleges, universities, churches, retreats and conferences. The most frequently asked question I hear after sharing with a group is, "What can we do? How can simplicity be realized in my life?"

How many CDs or DVDs can I have and still be simple? Can I own a laptop and simultaneously view my lifestyle as simple? How many unread books can I have in my library before I'm not celebrating simplicity? Are there certain neighborhoods or zip codes that are better to live in if I want to remain simple? Is it OK to have a savings account? What about investing? What kind of car does simplicity allow me to drive?

The fact that I'm even able to ask these questions presupposes certain things about conversations on simplicity. I was recently reminded of this while reading Douglas Coupland's novel *JPod*. "People who advocate simplicity," Coupland, a cultural critic, notes, "have money in the bank; the money came first, not the simplicity."[13] Sure, this might not always be the case, but for my friends who are poor, Coupland's statement sure sounds true. It seems like, in our struggle to find our way to simplicity, lots of our "stuff" gets in the way.

David Shi's work *The Simple Life* examines the historical culture of simplicity in America. He filters through the social framework that asks and seeks to answer these questions. His conclusion is,

> Simplicity in its essence demands neither a vow of poverty nor a life of rural homesteading. As an ethic of self-conscious material moderation, it can be practiced in cities and suburbs, townhouses and condominiums. It requires neither a log cabin nor a hairshirt but a deliberate ordering of priorities so as to distinguish between the necessary and superfluous, useful and wasteful, beautiful and vulgar.[14]

All of these are good questions, and Shi's conclusions are pacifying observations, but most of the questions, and most of the typical answers, are about what we have, want, or need. I wonder if the questions shouldn't be more about what *others* don't have, still want and desperately need.

But these sorts of questions often make us *feel* bad. Then we're at risk of being motivated to figure out a simplicity that is actually narcissistic. I've always appreciated Richard Foster's staple read on the topic, *Freedom of Simplicity*, especially the warning about our tendency to turn simplicity against itself. He writes, "Most dangerous of all is our tendency to turn any expressions of simplicity into a new legalism."[15] Well, now I'm in big trouble. Simplicity for simplicity's sake is really only legalism—that tyrannical feast of appearances where we put on airs to impress one another. David Chronic writes, "Attaching to Jesus leads to detaching from the world and to simplicity of lifestyle. This is not simplicity for the sake of simplicity, but simplicity for the sake of relationship—relationship with God and relationship with each other."[16]

When we embrace simplicity for simplicity's sake, we wind up smelling foul, inauthentic. The spirit of true simplicity, however, is redemptive. We see Jesus laying down his life. We see Jesus celebrating the One who gives everything. We see Jesus forgoing nonvalues as he embraces the true values of the kingdom of God.

This is what the prophet Isaiah was pointing to in his writings on the aspects of true fasting (Isaiah 58). Isaiah suggests that fasting isn't simply to go without food, but to take that food and feed the hungry with it. True fasting is meant to create an openness and emptiness in us to allow those on the margins to have their needs met and fulfilled, to clothe the naked and offer a place for the wanderer to stay.

Growing up, I really messed up fasting. I used to think of it as a way to manipulate God, sort of like putting God in a wrestling submission hold (not unlike a spiritual half-nelson-chicken-wing or a figure-four-leg-lock). I wanted fasting to make God do something for me—I wanted it to force God to answer my prayers. If I don't eat, then "God, you better hear my prayers, and you better answer them! Just look at me, so pathetic and miserable in my hunger." Fasting became the puppet strings fastened to God's arms and legs, and my going without food was supposed to give me the power to pull on those strings.

Isaiah deconstructs that paradigm and reconstructs one built around justice. The prophet shows us that voluntarily going without something, making a sacrifice, is ultimately for God to be able to answer the prayers of someone else who is forced to go without.

This seems to be where the two cousins, simplicity and voluntary poverty, connect. This has to do with our view of God. Raniero Cantalamessa suggests, "The Old Testament introduces us to a God who is 'for the poor,' while the New Testament shows us a God who Himself becomes poor."[17]

Saint Francis of Assisi embodied this as well as anyone. Moving from abundance to simplicity to poverty, Francis lived his sacrifice redemptively as an expression of his love for God. His biographer Omer Englebert writes, "Voluntarily poor one may be from philosophy or asceticism, for reasons of zeal, of charity, and others still.

But Francis was poor from love. He made himself poor because his beloved Christ had been poor."[18]

Francis lived this with such integrity that it became his stand which validated his message. This commitment to simplicity and poverty qualified and quantified his message: "Christ's teaching contains two different levels or forms of poverty: one required of everyone in order to *enter* the Kingdom, the other required of a few in particular in order to *announce* the Kingdom."[19]

THE GRACE IN USED PACIFIERS

I was on my way to the airport one morning, going to speak at a university's missions conference. I stopped by the Word Made Flesh office to check my mail and found a large envelope on my desk. I opened it up and found inside it a handful of used pacifiers. Since I was in a hurry to catch my flight, I put the envelope back on my desk and continued opening the rest of my mail.

Daphne Eck, a dear friend and coworker, saw the pacifiers and was intrigued. She asked if she could read the letter. She called Phileena over, and the two of them, after reading and rereading the letter, were moved to tears.

Realizing I missed something, I picked the letter up and read it. It said:

> I am sending you something a little "random." Our 2-year-old daughter Grace and I have a little prayer book that we pray through each night. Included in it are pictures of children who are sick, hurting, and alone. Recently, as we have been praying for these children and others like them in the world, Grace has been adamant about sending them her "bobbies." She has even picked out which children will receive which colors that will make them feel "all better." Even though she no longer uses her pacifiers, she is attached to them—she re-

members that they always make her feel better. They really are precious to her. I have told her that we will send them to hurting children just like the ones in her prayer book. I want her not only to experience sacrifice for others, but I want to also encourage her awareness of the needs and hurts of others. Please accept these on behalf of the children you encounter and know that there is a 2-year-old in Alabama who sincerely loves and prays for them.

I called everyone in the office together and read the letter aloud. We were all broken. Grace was only two years old, but she already figured it out. She knew that "by detaching ourselves from ourselves and attaching ourselves to God, by resisting the depreciation of our valuables and renouncing ourselves before God, and by rejecting a Pharisaic spirituality of pious comparisons and embracing a lifestyle rooted in our own poverty, we can truly celebrate simplicity for the sake of God and for the sake of humanity."[20]

It's not what you give—it's what you keep. As I left to speak, Grace's example inspired me to share about the revolution of love, the need to give all so that God's Kingdom can come. We have been given so much. Learning to loosen the grasp of our lives, our possessions, our hopes and dreams, our futures, and allowing God to take control is the entryway to simplicity in its purest form.

Two-year-old Grace, like the widow, like Deepa, gave everything. Nothing was left over; all was given to God.

4. SUBMISSION

I'm afraid of dogs.

When we were younger, my brothers and I used to fill the back-yard up with neighborhood friends for some pretty cut-throat games of kickball and wiffle-ball. We would pick teams and then face off in some of the most epic neighborhood sporting events of all time. ESPN Classic would have made a fortune off of us.

Hitting or kicking the ball over the fence was an automatic out because it meant we would have to trick our neighbor's dogs to get our ball back. An unlucky, usually smaller kid would be volunteered to go to the backyard of the home two houses down, where he would kick the fence to get the attention of the dog. The dog would bark and jump at this kid, turning its back to all of us waiting in my backyard. An even unluckier kid would then be volunteered to jump over the fence to get the ball before the dog realized it had been tricked. Needless to say, the dogs that lived on both sides of our home didn't have much love for us.

One summer afternoon, there was a small crowd of kids in the middle of my backyard picking teams. Our next-door neighbor to the south let their dog, Lobo, out of their backdoor. Lobo noticed his gate and our gate were both opened and sprinted out of his yard into ours, causing a panic as little kids screamed and ran for swing sets, the shed, and fences to climb.

My youngest brother, Drew, the smallest then, got caught, and Lobo bit him hard in the butt. It was ugly. All the kids were traumatized. Lobo's owner, in broken English, reiterated, "Lobo, he no bite," trying to convince us that my little brother's bleeding butt was perhaps from sliding into second base.

Since then I've remained a bit traumatized. Even little dogs scare me; they seem to give me the most trouble, actually. And yet strangely enough, it seems like dogs are drawn to me. Maybe they smell my fear. Whatever it is, dogs usually want my attention and go to all lengths to get it—including the always predictable attempt to nestle their nose into my crotch.

One evening, Phileena and I were having dinner at a friend's home. They have a big dog that seems gentle, but really scares me. This dog always tries to get my attention, and that particular night she walked right up to me, laid down at my feet, rolled halfway over on her back, and bared her hairy chest upward toward me.

I wasn't sure what to do. My friend told me to scratch her chest. Right. As if I'd fall for that trick. Let's see, how about I just put my hand right down there by her chin so she can bite it right off! Hmmm . . . I'll pass.

But my friend insisted, reassuring me that the dog was submitting to me, baring its most tender body part as a sign that she was vulnerable—woundable.

Suddenly the concept of submission made sense.

WEAK IN THE KNEES

I would say that I'm a fairly transparent person. Ask me just about anything you want and I typically have no problem opening up the tender parts of my heart. I am also very forthcoming with my feelings when I can get in touch with them. It's no surprise that I make lots of mistakes and usually don't have any trouble acknowledging my errors and making amends for them. But transparency isn't vulnerability.

Dogs are, essentially, always transparent. Except for those shameful occasions when people dress their dogs in sweaters, dogs are always naked as the day they were born. You always see them in toto, so to speak. Moreover, they communicate at a primal level: when they're happy, they wag their tail; when they're hungry, they drool; when they're angry, they growl. Dogs are transparent to the core. Vulnerability, by contrast, is an act of a dog's will. A dog makes a cognitive progression from their baseline of transparency to baring themselves to another. For me, being vulnerable is much more difficult than being transparent. I have a hard time exposing the parts of me that can be wounded. Sure, I can *share* my feelings with someone, but it's tough for me to *trust* people with my feelings. It's not easy for me to put my needs out there and give someone a chance to reject them. And so what I usually do is work toward transparency as a distraction from my lack of vulnerability.

There's no submission in that. Submission is giving up oneself to the power of another; transparency doesn't require submission because it sets the agenda of what I want to share. Transparency isn't an act of submission so much as it is a preemptive strike—a self-protecting attempt to keep people at a safe distance. Transparency in this way becomes an attempt to protect and control. Submission is a celebration not of insipid acquiescence but of confident surrender. Submission is an opportunity to affirm our deep trust in God by allowing God to be in control as we resist the urge to assert ourselves as God. I've come to learn that becoming vulnerable is submitting to others the deeper parts of my life.

Submission goes beyond vulnerability and becomes an expression of love. An invitation to intimacy. A release of control. In his book *Intimacy,* Henri Nouwen writes, "Love asks for a total disarmament."

Can we ever meet a fellow [human] without any protection? Reveal ourselves to [them] in our total vulnerability? Are man and woman able to exclude the power in their relationship and become totally available for each other? When the soldier sits down to eat he lays down his weapons, because eating means peace and rest. When he stretches out his body to sleep he is more vulnerable than ever. Table and bed are the two places of intimacy where love can manifest itself in weakness. In love men and women take off all the forms of power, embracing each other in total disarmament. The nakedness of their body is only a symbol of total vulnerability and availability.[1]

This is true in my relationship with God. God wants total disarmament from me. My prayers, by contrast, are usually full of requests and confessions. I admit my mistakes and instead of asking for more grace, I typically ask for the ability not to make the same mistake again. Rather than throwing myself on my real need for forgiveness, I try to reassure God that I'll do better next time. It's more about what I can do to please God than it is about what God has done to meet my needs. But for me to admit my need means that I'm dependent on and vulnerable to God. It strikes at the illusion of my self-sufficiency.

DISFIGURED SUBMISSION

As I've reflected on this, I've discovered a few malformations that have fortified this lack of submissive vulnerability in my relationships with friends and with God.

How I understand vulnerability and submission has been influenced by some distasteful cultural distortions. Traditional roles and relationships modeled between rich and poor, the powerful and powerless, clergy and laity, men and women, and husbands and wives have made submission unpleasant. The rich are tempted to allocate power according to what they own ("I am what I have"), so that submitting to friends who are poor in any sense is an absurd notion. Humanity is tempted to assimilate into the social organization handed to us ("I am what other people think about me"), so we cede power to the clergy and dismiss ourselves from a full responsibility to God. We observe differences in gender and accept social constructs of what is appropriate regarding those differences ("I am what I do"), not recognizing the groundwork that other power dynamics have already laid that affect the question.

Much of my time is spent with people who are very poor. I consider many of them friends and family. Stories they've told me are unbelievable—children forced to amputate the hands or legs of their own parents before taking up arms and fighting in civil wars; physical and sexual abuse so nightmarish that it drives a five- or six-year-old to the streets; women and children enslaved through sex-trafficking and subsequently raped in the brothels that are now their homes/prisons.

The submission of people who are poor to those who are rich shocks me. I can't understand it. Why don't these women stand up to the pimps and brothel owners that exploit them? Why don't they refuse sex from the men who climb on top to rape them?

Phyllis Kilbourn, in her book *Street Children: A Guide to Effective Ministry*, writes about E. P. Seligman's research on learned helplessness.[2] Seligman put a dog in a cage, rang a bell, then sent electric current through the cage to shock the dog. Of course the dog yelped and barked and did everything possible to escape, but couldn't. Pretty sick and sad too. After this procedure had been executed a number of times, the researcher started to see a trend. Now when the bell rang, the dog curled up and laid down. The dog had learned helplessness. There was nothing it could do but suffer through the pain. The researcher then took the top of the cage off so the dog could freely escape, rang the bell and sent the electricity to the cage. Instead of jumping out to painless bliss and freedom, the dog laid down and took it.

We see this sort of learned helplessness a lot among our friends. For such a long time they have been oppressed and repressed.

Forced to submit to those with power.

Forced to work for unjust and low wages.

Forced to participate in dehumanizing activities.

Forced to live on the streets, in red-light districts, in refugee camps, in slums.

Even when given a chance to assume a position of power over their own lives, or even over their oppressors, many of them remain submitted to the pain dealt to them. Wealth and power become a false idol that demands submission.

THE PROBLEM OF POWER

Power dynamics are at work in the church too. Growing up in the Catholic Church, I admired the priests and thought they were larger than life. Their vestments and proficiency with liturgy seemed to put a great amount of distance between them and the rest of us "regular" people.

When my parents started attending church at an evangelical, Protestant congregation, there were lots of changes, but the rock-star image of our pastors seemed pretty familiar. At the Protestant church the pastors didn't dress up in religious clothes and weren't very interested in liturgical ceremony, but they protected their approachability and availability through their secretaries and interns. Their time seemed precious, almost too precious for "normal" people.

Now the guys who ran both the Catholic and Protestant churches I grew up in were extremely humble and sincere. And in both traditions the ideal is that the clergy would posture themselves submissively in their desire to serve those they minister among. But in lots of cases, becoming a leader in a church simply aggravates an inflated view of self and creates new repressive expressions of submission. These power dynamics are manifested in gender relationships as well. You've probably read or heard the often quoted statement, "Women constitute one half of the world's population, they do two-thirds of the world's work, they earn one tenth of the world's income and they own one hundredth of the world's property including land."[3] What's the deal? Can't we figure this one out?

The disparity between women and men is shamefully obvious, and the deformation of submission in relationships between men and women has a long history. Sadly, women have historically and culturally been defined by their relationships with men. It's her father, husband or children (in many cultures, preferably sons) that ascribe value and identity to a woman. This of course has created all sorts of opportunities for exploitation and repression.

The church has been complicit in all of this. Sue Monk Kidd was a dutiful and submissive wife of a Baptist preacher. She had a very conservative religious view of herself as a woman and allowed that to shape her identity. Then she entered a process, considered scandalous by some, of coming to terms with her humanity. She bravely documents her journey in the book *Dance of the Dissident Daughter*, challenging the assumption that women, simply because of their gender, are obligated to submit to men.

> With men at the top (or at least with a sense of entitlement about being at top) and women below (or at least with a sense of belonging below), a way of relating was put into place based on dominance and dependence. The role of the one above was to dominate and oversee the ones below. The role of the one below was to answer to and depend on the one above. In addition, the one above learned how to protect his prestigious place at the top. He learned to stay up by keeping her down, that is, by insisting she be content with things as they are.[4]

Kidd's voice is so important because in nearly every culture throughout history women have been forced to submit to men with little or no reciprocity. Christians are among the worst violators of this practice. The early church had a hard time figuring out if women had souls and, if so, whether or not they could be saved.[5] Conservative churches have argued that the Bible has clearly defined gender roles that must be maintained.

Of course Sue Monk Kidd's conclusions aren't new and she's not the only one to have made them. But sadly, in an age when we can single out fanatics or groups like the Taliban for their repressive attitude toward women, we still have a hard time seeing our own complicity. We cringe at the thought of covering women with a burka. At the same time our culture creates tremendous pressure for women to wear a "burka of flawless beauty": perfect complexions, stunningly white teeth, even straight smiles, tastefully made-up faces, and bodies that are flawless.[6] Desmond Tutu puts it this way:

> The Bible is quite clear that the divine image is constitutive of humanity irrespective of gender. I cannot be opposed to racism, in which people are discriminated against as a result of something about which they can do nothing—their skin color—and then accept with equanimity the gross injustice of penalizing others for something else they can do nothing about—their gender.[7]

Christian talk of submission almost immediately implies the relationship between husbands and wives. Ephesians 5:21 reads, "Submit to one another out of reverence for Christ." The next verse, Ephesians 5:22, simply reiterates what Paul has already written, "Wives, submit to your husbands as to the Lord."[8]

Paul actually places the weight and ultimate responsibility of submission on the husband. Both the husband and wife are called to a posture of mutual submission, but verses 25-33 explain that the husband is commanded further to love as "Christ loved the church and gave himself up for her" (Ephesians 5:25). One doesn't get more vulnerable than that.

What does this kind of submission look like? It's a love that cleanses and purifies (5:26-27); it's an instinctive love a man naturally has for himself (verse 28); it's a love that surrenders self-interest for the other (verse 29); it's a love that cares (verse 29); and it's a love that is loyal (verse 31).

Ultimately, it is a reflection of the love that Christ has for the church. "We love," 1 John 4:19 reads, "because Christ first loved us." When we know he loves us, it's nearly impossible not to love him back—and that's exactly what Paul writes when he closes the passage.

Unfortunately, most young Christians learn about submission from repression in marriage. And if Christian tradition requires the wife to submit without a reciprocal submission from the husband, then we've been misled. And eventually this misperception leads to theological repression of women by malforming our understanding of female dignity and identity. This has played itself out in the unbalanced church of women led by men, in marriages where a wife's voice is secondary to that of her husband, and even in many areas of nonreligious society where women's contributions in the workplace, family and social sectors go unrecognized or downplayed. Given this patriarchal conditioning, how can we free ourselves from this inherited assumption bent toward power and control?

C. S. Lewis suggests that this love is embodied

> not in the husband we should all wish to be but *in him whose marriage is most like a crucifixion*; whose wife receives most and gives least, is most unworthy of him, is—*in her own mere nature*—least lovable. For the Church has no beauty but what the Bridegroom gives her. He does not find, but makes her, lovely.[9]

Though Lewis's reflections may logically be consistent with the metaphor of the cross, his concept suggests that the husband intrinsically enters a marriage as morally superior, thus fortifying socially repressive gender norms. The nuances of vulnerable submission are present, but I'm left asking, how can man *and* woman, husband *and* wife embody the love present on the cross? How does the cross translate submission motivated by love for us today?

Submission isn't a wife dutifully serving an uncaring husband. Submission isn't a child being forced to obey against his will. Submission is a voluntary expression of love. Submission is carrying the cross that signifies Christlike love, and a cross that is redemptive. Submission is the indication that love is sincere. Submission is the extension of a love that gives all without expectation of any return.

Fundamentally, submission deals with power relationships. And in practice, who submits to whom is usually an indication of who has more authority.

Authority, sadly, has been misused in nearly every area in which it is leveraged. I have seen the abuse of authority all around the world, observing the relationships between adults and children, husbands and wives, the rich and the poor, the powerful and the powerless. I have seen how governments and economies levy authority against the good of the people these institutions exist to serve. I have even seen the church misuse its authority over its membership, often breaking the hearts and confusing the faith of the fellow believers.

SACRIFICE AND SUBMISSION

Francis Bacon's musings on power are thoughtfully provocative: "It is a strange desire to seek power and to lose liberty; or to seek power over others and to lose power over [one]'s self."[10] Power in and of itself can in fact be a gift to the one who obtains it—when it's relinquished. Many in my community have embodied what's good in this, seeking power and influence to change what keeps our friends poor. It's quite overwhelming in fact. In some ways, through our solidarity with those who are poor, we have limited our own freedoms. Some of us, for example, have promised to care for children that aren't ours, who will need families for the next eighteen years and beyond.

Jayakumar Christian explores the idea of power and submission through the text of Revelation 5:6-13:

> Then I saw a Lamb, looking as if it had been slain, standing in the center before the throne, encircled by the four living creatures and the elders. The Lamb had seven horns and seven eyes, which are the seven spirits of God sent out into all the earth. He went and took the scroll from the right hand of him who sat on the throne. And when he had taken it, the four living creatures and the twenty-four elders fell down before the Lamb. Each one had a harp and they were holding golden bowls full of incense, which are the prayers of God's people. And they sang a new song, saying:
>
> > "You are worthy to take the scroll
> > > and to open its seals,
> > because you were slain,
> > > and with your blood you purchased for God
> > > members of every tribe and language and people
> > > and nation.
> > You have made them to be a kingdom and priests
> > > to serve our God,
> > and they will reign on the earth."
>
> Then I looked and heard the voice of many angels, number-ing thousands upon thousands, and ten thousand times ten

thousand. They encircled the throne and the living creatures and the elders. In a loud voice were saying:

> "Worthy is the Lamb, who was slain,
> to receive power and wealth and wisdom and strength
> and honor and glory and praise!"

Then I heard every creature in heaven and on earth and under the earth and on the sea, and all that is in them, saying:

> "To him who sits on the throne and to the Lamb
> be praise and honor and glory and power,
> for ever and ever!'"

Christian notes that the kingdom of God "reverse[s] the so-called natural order and popular understanding of power."[11] In Revelation 5:6 this is illustrated by the lamb, but this is only one example of the biblical model of power reversal. God chooses a shepherd, David, to become king. Jesus chooses a child to teach us about greatness. In Revelation 5 the triumphant Lion of Judah enters the scene as a little slain lamb, suggesting that "in the hereafter, when the kingdom of God comes in its final glory, there will be reversals in the natural order and the popular understanding of power." Christian goes on to note that "the slain Lamb *is* the paradigm of power" in the kingdom of God.[12]

This is revolutionary. Professional sports teams, universities and colleges, even governments often adopt a mascot or unifying symbol to rally people around. These mascots and symbols almost without exception exude some form of power and intimidation. We know them well—the Lions, Rams, Falcons, Bears, Gators, Wildcats and Hurricanes. But lambs? Seriously? "The slain Lamb reverses the world's understanding of power to make it look like powerlessness."[13] The image of a slain Lamb is symbolic of complete vulnerability—a submission that opens itself to the ultimate sacrifice.

Revelation 5:9 highlights the song sung around the throne of this slain lamb. In this song, we learn that God has redeemed people "from every tribe and language and people and nation." This goes against much of what we have come to believe about power. In today's present reality, power often hints at fear and control. But in this biblical portrait of reality, power isn't something that adults use against children, men use against women, and the rich use against people who are poor. In this reality, God's power is accessible to all those who submit themselves to God. A kingdom perception of power lays down all possibility of control that excludes others and opens us to the possibility of a new submission.

In Revelation 5:12-13, the song to the Lamb validates that all true power is God's power. Christian writes, "In the kingdom of God all expressions of power will affirm the theocentric nature of the kingdom."[14] This requires us to reevaluate how we perceive power. If all power affirms the glory of God, if all power leads to the praise and honor of God, and if all power belongs to God, then what we have understood as power today is actually oppression.

Those unjustly exploited can legitimately raise the question of whether God is good; their pain validates the accusation and the uncertainty. However, no pain could be greater than the pain God feels on behalf of victims of exploitation. The vulnerability of Christ becomes a sign of his power embodied in his love.

This is one of the reasons I love Saint Francis of Assisi. He offers a different example. Francis was larger than life. Before his conversion he was a popular playboy in his small Italian town. Well loved by nearly everyone, Francis was a natural leader with an incredible amount of charisma.

The story goes that to prove himself, Francis went off to fight in a local feud that his village ultimately lost. He was taken as a prisoner of war and held for a year before his poor health helped secure his release.

On his journey home, humiliated and defeated, Francis encountered a man with leprosy. Resisting every urge within himself to turn away, Francis got down off his horse, embraced and clothed that man, and discovered Christ. It was a conversion experience that propelled this energetic and playful youth into the contemplative mystic he would eventually become.

Spending countless hours praying in a small dilapidated church on the hillside of his village, Francis heard Christ call him to "rebuild my church which is in ruins." Francis initially thought this meant actually rebuilding a physical structure, and so he spent a couple of years restoring a number of old churches in the Spoletto Valley before he realized that his calling was to bring his neighbors who were poor back to the center of the church's community.

Francis committed this to prayer and in a relatively short amount of time built quite a large community around himself. This new order gained exceptional popularity and Francis found himself the leader of something bigger than anyone could ever have imagined.

He could have laid claim to an enormous amount of power. But he didn't. He kept it simple. He begged for his food, and when he saw people with older or moldier bread than his, Francis would exchange his food with theirs.

He could have dressed himself up in the most lavish vestments, but Francis would himself become naked to cover those on the streets who had nothing to wear.

Certainly, as the head of a religious order, Francis's time demands were substantial, but he always made time for the stranger, the young, people begging and especially those with leprosy.

One of my favorite stories is when Francis went to the woods looking for one of his companions, Friar Bernard. After having called out to Friar Bernard three times without a response, Francis presumed that Bernard was ignoring him. Frustrated, Francis went away to pray. In prayer it was revealed to him that Friar Bernard was so enraptured in contemplation that he had never even heard Francis calling him.

Humbled, Francis returned to the place where Friar Bernard had been praying and commanded him to submit to an act of penance. Bernard had no choice but to submit to Francis's request. Francis laid on his back and said, "To punish my presumption and the arrogance of my heart . . . you shall set one foot on my throat and the other on my mouth and so pass over me three times."[15] Are you serious? Walk on St. Francis's face? Though a man of authority, Francis humbled himself and gave his power back to his community—a true model of submission in every way.

ENTITLEMENT AND SUBMISSION

When I was around eleven years old, I got awfully sick. I was usually healthy, but one evening I was out with some friends riding bikes when a headache sent me home.

Pain has always been a motivator in my life—a challenge I try to overcome—but that evening I recall finding it strange that I was allowing pain to prevent me from doing something that I was enjoying. Nonetheless, I went home and was in bed before the sun set that Friday night.

My parents found me the next morning nearly paralyzed. My head was literally killing me. It hurt to lay my head on a pillow. I was in deep distress and experiencing the most intense pain I've known. Mom and Dad rushed me to the doctor. After a series of tests, the doctor informed my parents that I was dying. I was rushed into surgery. It's all glimpses, like a dream, in my memory, but I can't forget the pain of the needle that they used to perform a spinal tap. After that, I slipped into a coma.

Even though I was unconscious, I remember things that happened while in the coma. I remember my dad staying with me that night, and I even remember what he watched on the TV in my hospital room.

The doctors informed my parents that I had viral spinal meningitis and encephalitis. They said there was a 70 percent chance that I wouldn't live. They said if I did live, I would be in the coma for at least three weeks. They couldn't promise anything. If I survived the coma, it was likely that I would be blind and deaf, severely brain damaged, and paralyzed from the neck down.

The pastor of the church my parents were attending came to the hospital. It was the third day of my sickness. I was still in the coma. He sat beside me and prayed for me.

I woke up. There was an old man with gray hair praying for me. I was hooked up to all kinds of medical equipment that I didn't know anything about. I was embarrassed because I had wet the bed and there was a room full of people staring at me.

During the next couple days, more than fifteen doctors and interns examined me. It was a miracle. I was completely healed and left the hospital without a single side effect.

As a child, I didn't know how to fully appreciate what I went through and how God had given me a second chance at life. It took several years for the sobering reality of that event to sink in. Today I can hardly gather my thoughts when I try to understand that the breath in my lungs is a reminder of a life that was almost lost. Through this experience I have come to accept that my life is not my own—it's God's and I not only want to, but need to, serve God with it.

The truth is, no one really "owns" their own life—every breath is a gift from God. And once we become aware of this notion that our life is not our own, submitting our life to God is an obvious response. Awareness of God's grace creates an opportunity to submit who we are, what we are and all that we might become to God.

Samuel Kamaleson illustrates this concept in a Christian folk story from South India.[16] There are several versions of it, but here it opens with a young boy who loved to play marbles. He regularly walked through his neighborhood with a pocketful of his best marbles, hoping to find opponents to play against. One marble in particular, his special blue marble, had won him many matches.

During one walk he encountered a young girl who was eating a bag of chocolate candy. Though the boy's first love was marbles, he had a weakness for chocolates. As he stood there interacting with the young girl, his salivary glands and the rumbling in his stomach became uncontrollable, and he thought to himself, *I have got to get my hands on those chocolates.*

Concocting a plan, he asked the girl, "How about I give you all these marbles for those chocolates?" She replied, "Sounds fair to me."

He put his hand in his pocket, searching for the distinguishing cracks on the surface of the blue marble. Once he identified the blue marble with his finger tip, he carefully pushed it to the bottom of his pocket and pulled out all the other marbles.

As he handed the marbles to the girl in exchange for the chocolates, the boy thought his plan was a success and turned to walk away. As he began to eat the candy, he suddenly turned to the girl and asked, "Hey, did you give me *all* the chocolates?"

Our fallen nature persuades us to posture ourselves in the same deceptive and defiant attitude as the boy in this story. We want everything the kingdom of God has to offer. We want to have a secure sense of God's presence, we want all our prayers to be answered, we want to "feel close" to Jesus, we want to flourish in the riches of God's glory—we want it all. But we are unwilling to give up everything for it. Many times there is a "blue marble" in our lives that we seem unwilling to offer to the control of Christ. Until we can fully subjugate ourselves to God's will, our participation in God's kingdom will be limited.

How sad and ironic that we expect God to give us all in return for only a portion of what God asks from us. The kingdom of God is a treasure, and to acquire the fullness of all that is there, we must give up everything, submitting our lives to God's control.

SUBMISSION AND SERVICE

This realization caught up to me one afternoon while I was taking classes in Jerusalem. God used Bob Marley—the "Legend"—to help me realize my call to submission through service.

I was hanging out on campus with some friends. We were outside in the garden enjoying a sunny afternoon. In the background, someone was playing *Talkin' Blues,* a Bob Marley CD with ten interviews slipped in between songs.[17] I found myself captivated with these candid excerpts and listened closely to what he had to say. Themes of the interview clips and songs ranged from slavery to life in the slum to oppression.

Something in my heart grew anxious. It was like the feeling you have just before you jump off the diving board—a bit nervous, a little excited, but overall restless.

Later on, several students gathered together for an evening devotion. The Scripture read that night came from Luke 8:26-39, the story of a man possessed by a legion of demons. The story goes like this: Jesus gets in a boat and crosses a lake, where he's met by a crazy man living in a graveyard. This man has been chained; he cries out day and night, he even cuts himself with stones. The man is possessed. It must have been terrifying. But Jesus doesn't look at the terror. He looks through it and sees a tender heart that he loves.

Interestingly, the man recognizes Christ. In the parallel account of this passage in Mark 5:1-20, the Scriptures tell us that from a distance he sees Jesus and runs to him. The introductions are a little strained. "What do you want with me, Jesus?" abruptly starts the dialogue. Jesus just wants a name. "Legion" is the name given, because of the army of demons harassing the man. Jesus sends the demons into a herd of pigs; the pigs start a stampede and follow each other into the lake where they all drown. The people working with the pigs run to the nearby town and tell everyone what has just happened. Some of the people have to see it with their own eyes. When they show up, the man who had been tormented by the demons is in his right mind. The people are afraid and ask Christ to leave.

That's some crazy stuff. I had read through that story countless times, but that night the Scripture seemed alive. The story unfolded in my mind with a couple Bob Marley songs as a background soundtrack.

That *Talkin' Blues* album, it turns out, was an excellent Bible commentary. The possessed man in Luke 8 is chained in a similar way to how many in the Majority World are bound by injustice. He cries out day and night in solidarity with those today who cry out in their anguish. He cuts himself as a victim of unseen forces in the same way that some people who are poor today commit violent acts, use drugs and enter into prostitution as part of the drama they've been conscripted into. He lives in the tombs just as those on the margins today are banished to slums and ghettos.

The passage, incidentally, begins with an act of submission: Jesus leaves a familiar place and goes to *the other side*. He risks being misunderstood, rejected and even wounded. By leaving Galilee he shows us that we have to follow him into the world, to the oppressed and poor.

Those who are poor and oppressed recognize Jesus when they see him, just as the man in Luke knew who Jesus was. He probably was already waiting for Christ to arrive. And yet when the man was freed, the people of the village were afraid and sent Jesus away. I sometimes think that many nonpoor Western Christians are afraid to see oppressed people liberated, because establishing justice is costly. The Jews were treated poorly by world governments even after the Holocaust. Native Americans were given the dustiest, driest, most barren wastelands as protected lands, or "reservations," by the U.S. government. African American descendants of those who were forced into slavery find themselves in some of contemporary society's most underfunded public schools.

Bob Marley, the voice of the oppressed, helped me to see my call to serving Jesus among those who are poor. The need he represented challenged me to submit myself to God, and in that submission to God I discovered the opportunity to submit to the cries and the needs of my friends who suffer.

SUBMITTING OR STEALING

I don't always submit. This was made painfully clear to me one afternoon in Lima, Peru. We were playing soccer in a park with a group of street children and I was getting used. These kids were mostly undernourished, and lots of them had been smoking glue bags throughout the game to distract themselves from the pain of their reality. Still, they were having their way with me. I was getting frustrated and wishing the game would end when the distraction I needed passed right in front of my face.

Manolito ran right through the middle of the playing field, interrupting our game. I had met him just recently. He lived with his common-law wife in a slum where they were trying to raise their newborn baby. He was a quiet guy—sensitive, soft-spoken and generally reserved. A caring father, he was still really a boy trying to figure out who he was. As he ran through the park he was wearing a purple and green windbreaker inside out. The jacket looked brand new against his dirty skin and the rest of his street-worn, dingy clothing. As he ran past us, my good friend Walter asked him why he was running. Manolito's reply was abrupt as he kept running, glancing over his shoulder in the direction from where he had come.

I asked Walter why Manolito was running and why he didn't seem to want to play soccer with the rest of the kids. Walter's response was a short-lived, quickly fulfilled prediction: Manolito had probably stolen the jacket and was running to get away from the victim of the crime. Just as Walter finished answering my question, a Peruvian man, probably around twenty-five years old, ran through the park chasing Manolito.

My heart went out to the angry young man. I'm sure he liked that jacket and was probably minding his own business when it was taken from him. But as I watched the scene unfold, my heart also went out to Manolito. I found myself torn between hoping that the young man would get his jacket back and hoping that Manolito would have something to keep him warm as he spent another cold night on the streets of Lima.

It was a complex encounter concerning some crucial issues of justice, submission and identity. Manolito had stolen what he needed—a jacket to keep his cold body warm or perhaps to sell when his empty stomach could no longer take the hunger pangs. The Peruvian man seemed to be the victim, but upon my reflection, he—and even I—seemed to be a thief as well.

When we don't submit our lives to God and our possessions to people in need, when we mistake our financial and material blessings as personal provision rather than as resources with potential for kingdom development—have we perpetuated an unjust imbalance between us and our neighbors? Could it be that our deformed perceptions of power, our selfish tendencies to accumulate and hoard, cause many of the world's poor to go without their basic needs?

It seems to me that we are thieves when we hold onto those things that don't actually belong to us. It seems to me that God has intended some of "our" things for friends who are poor. It may be our education, our savings account, maybe even our ability to choose our occupation or the neighborhood where we live. Many times it's our very life. Could the things we value the most be occasions for biblical reciprocity—ways for the nonpoor to submit to those on the margins and in need?

Our theft of God's blessing and provision does not, of course, justify the crimes poor people may sometimes commit. But neither does our naïve presumption of God's goodness justify the criminal attitudes we foster and the felonious postures of our hearts. May Manolito's theft challenge us to consider the disobedience we perpetuate through our own disregard for our sisters, brothers and neighbors in need. May Manolito's witness cause us to reevaluate all that God has placed into our hands. May Manolito's vulnerability to an oppressive poverty call us back to a true, vulnerable love, responsive to our neighbor and fully submitted to the One who made us and gave us everything.

5. BROKENNESS

There was a distinct pattern of table manners that Jesus seemed to employ at critical moments throughout his life. It happened once when Jesus fed five thousand men, not including the women and children (Matthew 14:15-21). It happened again when Jesus fed four thousand (Matthew 15:29-39). It happened yet again during the Last Supper (Matthew 26:20-35). Finally, it happened on the road to Emmaus (Luke 24:13-32).

Bread always seemed to be available, and eyes always seemed to need to be opened.

The verbs used and reused in all these stories make it easy to see the pattern. Jesus would take bread, bless it, break it and give it. Not that profound—in fact, something that many of us do on a regular basis. But what happened when Jesus took bread, blessed it, broke it and then gave it changed the world.

Some of us know what the bread feels like. We've experienced brokenness in hurt relationships or in disappointments, in loneliness or in moments when we've felt misunderstood. Many of us may carry the hurts and wounds of brokenness for our entire lives.

Others of us, however, still need to experience brokenness. We are proud, selfish, independent and arrogant. Until such things are broken at the feet of Jesus, our capacity to fully worship God remains bottled up. We need to become like the woman who broke an expensive jar of perfume so that she could anoint Jesus' feet—the wages of her sin broken in exchange for Jesus' healing (John 12:1-7). Our refusal to be broken by our sin leads us down the path of Judas, who hid his greed and theft and foreshadowed his betrayal even as he protested the woman's act.

Brokenness is different from *woundedness*. Woundedness is the impact of the inevitable pains shared by humanity, the internalization of human pain and the way it plays out in our self-perceptions, relationships and human interaction. Brokenness is different—a voluntary surrender to God's will over our own will. Woundedness is reactive, largely determined by how we respond to difficult or painful things that happen. Brokenness is open even to the grace in pain. Brokenness is *proactive*.

Being broken can be something that happens to us, but it can also be something we allow to happen in us, for in the broken areas of our lives Jesus can fill us with himself.

TAKING OUT THE TRASH

One of the things I hate the most is seeing someone eat from the trash. As Phileena and I have visited the corners of the world, we always seem to stumble across someone going through the garbage to find something to eat.

I have amazing and vivid memories of Havana, Cuba. Almost immediately upon our arrival we were confronted with the repression Cubans face daily. The working poor can never get ahead—the consequences and impacts of a longstanding economic embargo. Though one of the most repressed cities in the world, it nevertheless has to be among the world's dreamiest and most romantic.

One afternoon, as we sat at a little sidewalk café to grab a quick lunch, we noticed a dignified older black man, dressed nicely in a short-sleeved, collared red shirt, a stylish straw hat, pleated pants and old-school black-and-white wingtips. Like most Cubans, he was probably highly educated. Deep wrinkles were carved into his worn face. I was enjoying a cup of stiff espresso as he stopped at a large, industrial garbage container and opened the lid.

My first reaction was disgust—I was sitting downwind, and the cool breeze was blowing the rotten smell of trash into my face. The smell ruined the moment, but it was about to get worse. The man began digging through the trash.

First, he pulled out plastic and glass bottles to recycle. Then he started pulling out bits of wasted food from the café at which I sat. He set aside a piece of old dry bread and then what looked to be a soggy, half-eaten hamburger bun. I tried not to stare, as I'm sure he was humiliated, but I was mesmerized by sadness. That's what it means to be hungry.

The man put the bottles and the bits of food in an old shoulder bag, closed the lid to the container and walked away. As he went, he looked me in the eyes and, with his head held high, nodded. I'll never forget the look in his sad eyes.

That scenario has played out before me countless times. Men like him, as well as women and children all around the world, live off of what the rest of us waste. One of the first times I witnessed this kind of thing, I was in Kolkata. It was my first trip to the city back in 1993, the summer I worked at Mother Teresa's House for the Dying. That summer I would do anything I could to help: anything except take out the trash.

Now, it's not that I was a slacker. It's just that what we put into the trash was absolutely horrible. Everyone tried to avoid emptying the trash.

After the meals, whatever food wasn't eaten or was contaminated was thrown into the trash.

Some of the men and women who were admitted into the home had been on the streets for so long that it was nearly impossible to wash the grime and filth out of their clothes. Their soiled rags were thrown into the trash.

Many of the people who came to the home had so much lice in their hair and beards that they would be shaved bald. The infested piles of dark, black hair were thrown into the trash.

Old syringes that could not be sterilized and reused were thrown into the trash.

Nearly every patient had a little clay pot beside his bed to collect the bloody mucus he would spit up throughout the day. Once these clay pots were full, they were thrown into the trash.

Tuberculosis patients would fill tubs with vomit, blood and bits of their lungs. The contents of the tubs were thrown into the trash.

Whenever a patient would cough up a worm, it was immediately thrown into the trash.

We cleaned the cuts and removed the old dressings from the patients whose open wounds were filled with maggots or those patients who had leprosy. The dirty bandages would be thrown into the trash.

Each day the trash would be emptied four or five times. Two people would put a bamboo post through the wire loops on the rim of the trash can and start out the door toward a huge dumpsite two hundred yards away.

I could probably count the times on both hands that I took out the trash during those first seven weeks volunteering in the home. It took more of a toll on me than any other task I would set out to do during those days. In India, garbage piles are a common site for slum dwellings; the hill of waste serves as a sort of salvage center for very poor people. This dump was no exception. Surrounding the hill of trash were some of the poorest people and the most precious children I have ever seen.

We would take our trash can and pour it out on the hill of waste.

Before we could finish emptying it, four or five women would pick through it with sticks, looking for food or something they could recycle. On their hands and knees were naked children with bloated stomachs, picking through that wretched and miserable waste—children so hungry that they would begin eating the scraps of food and remains of fruit left on the mango pits.

The most horrible things you can imagine were in that trash, yet those people were so hungry they did not care. It made me sick to my stomach. I wanted to scream and cry every time I went out there. Even now, as I think back on it, my eyes are full of tears.

Those beautiful people were literally taking their life into their hands by putting things in their mouths that had come from inside a home full of death and disease. It is the epitome of degradation. And here I live in a country that throws away tons of consumable food every day.

God used those images redemptively to show me some of the false identities that I cling to. God has crowned us as princes and princesses in the kingdom. Too often we do not believe it, so we let our flesh go picking through the trash of the world for things like attention, affection, love—anything that will make us feel good about ourselves. When we're unwilling to recognize our true identity, God often shows us our false identity through the poverty of our friends.

BROKEN FOR WHOLENESS

Luke 14:16-24 tells of a great feast prepared by a king.

A certain man was preparing a great banquet and invited many guests. At the time of the banquet he sent his servant to tell those who had been invited, "Come, for everything is now ready."

But they all alike began to make excuses. The first said,

"I have just bought a field, and I must go and see it. Please excuse me."

Another said, "I have just bought five yoke of oxen, and I'm on my way to try them out. Please excuse me."

Still another said, "I just got married, so I can't come."

The servant came back and reported this to his master. Then the owner of the house became angry and ordered his servant, "Go out quickly into the streets and alleys of the town and bring in the poor, the crippled, the blind and the lame."

"Sir," the servant said, "what you ordered has been done, but there is still room."

Then the master told his servant, "Go out to the roads and country lanes and make them come in, so that my house will be full. I tell you, not one of those men who were invited will get a taste of my banquet."

In this parable Jesus is pointing out where some of his listeners need to be broken by pointing them toward those whose brokenness is on display. We are all invited to join this King at his table, but rather than taking our place at God's lavish banquet, many times we find ourselves sitting around on a heap of rotting garbage waiting for something to feed our false identities.

On a personal level, some of the movies, music and programs that we are entertained by are trash that only poisons our souls. The gossip and slander that slips through our lips is refuse that contaminates our hearts and minds. The negative and critical attitudes that we foster are festering cesspools that drown our character.

On a structural level, our own slavery to consumerism, nationalism and an entitled sense of self-worth feed something begging inside us with the trash that it yearns for. The leftovers of misunderstood readings of our own dignity and identity are lies that we stuff down the garbage chutes of our souls. Even some of the unhealthy relationships we find ourselves in become a form of trash that pollutes our minds and hearts. All of these sinful choices are trash that we feed ourselves.

Mother Teresa used to tell us of our need for the poor. As we are exposed to the suffering of neighbors who are poor, our own spiritual poverty comes more clearly into view. We are broken when we recognize our utmost need *for* God and leave everything behind to have our needs met *in* God. It's really that simple. As we see more and more of Jesus and learn to live in God's will, we will be free to stop picking through the trash and start living like the princes and princesses that we are.

C. S. Lewis's *Great Divorce* is an allegory of an imaginary place between heaven and hell. The central figure in this book boards a bus that's on its way to the outlands of heaven. Passengers are met by angels who are actually long-lost friends and family members from their pasts. Each encounter is a lesson of surrender and brokenness, as the passengers (who, we come to learn, are ghosts) are given a chance to leave behind the one thing that has kept them out of heaven, symbolized by a journey to the mountains.

In one of my favorite vignettes,[1] a ghost needs to be broken of his lust, depicted as a small, red lizard with a twitching tail like a whip. The little lizard sits on the shoulder of the ghost, whispering lies in the ghost's ear. An angel intervenes, volunteering to kill the lizard and free the ghost from this sin that has destroyed him. The ghost resists, knowing that he wants freedom but afraid of the pain that gaining his freedom will entail.

Eventually the ghost gives his permission, and the angel takes the red lizard, twisting it and breaking its back, and throwing it to the ground, where it writhes until it dies. Suddenly the ghost is physically transformed into a large, healthy man. Simultaneously the remains of the lizard are transformed into a living, beautiful stallion. The newly restored man jumps on the stallion and rides off to the mountains toward redemption.

The narrator asks his mentor about the nature of brokenness. The mentor replies,

> Nothing, not even the best and noblest, can go on as it now is. Nothing, not even what is lowest and most bestial, will not be raised again if it submits to death. It is sown a natural body, it is raised a spiritual body. Flesh and blood cannot come to the Mountains. Not because they are too rank, but because they are too weak. What is a lizard compared with a stallion? Lust is a poor, weak, whimpering, whispering thing compared with that richness and energy of desire which will arise when lust has been killed.[2]

God's brokenness creates wholeness. God is breaking those things in us that are twisted and wrong, destructive and sinful. Once broken, those things are then redeemed and restored to be used in their fullness for the glory of the kingdom of God.

BROKEN IN COMMUNITY

Henri Nouwen writes, "A person who in the eyes of others is broken suddenly is full of life, because you discover your own brokenness through them."[3] Our awareness of our brokenness moves us toward intimacy with Jesus; it becomes a place where we discover God's love for us, ushering us to a place of wholeness.

Brokenness is thus the sign of Jesus. He takes us broken and blesses us with community; in that community we are broken again and given to the world as agents of healing and redemption. Paradoxically, it is through brokenness that the kingdom of God is held together.

Brokenness in God's kingdom is always redemptive. Jesus takes bread, blesses it, breaks it and *gives* it. Once we've been taken and blessed, we then must be broken before we can truly be given.

There's a concept in chemistry called the "limiting capacity." An eight-ounce cup can only hold eight ounces of liquid. That is its limiting capacity. If the bottom of an eight-ounce cup is broken off, however, the limiting capacity is no longer a factor; that cup is capable of having an entire ocean poured *through* it.

This concept of limiting capacity applies similarly to people who are not yet broken by God. God's boundless and limitless love can be given to us and through us—as long as our posture is that of brokenness. This *spirituality of brokenness* is evident in the temptations of Christ, where we see him embrace his *broken identity*.

BROKEN AND BELOVED

Matthew 3:13–4:11 has to be one of the most sacred stories in Scripture; the narrative could have only come from the lips of Jesus. In an act of vulnerability Christ shared this story with us, one of his most trying times—possibly one of the most intimate experiences of his soul.

> Jesus came from Galilee to the Jordan to be baptized by John. But John tried to deter him, saying, "I need to be baptized by you, and do you come to me?"
>
> Jesus replied, "Let it be so now; it is proper for us to do this to fulfill all righteousness." Then John consented.
>
> As soon as Jesus was baptized, he went up out of the water. At that moment heaven was opened, and he saw the Spirit of God descending like a dove and alighting on him. And a voice from heaven said, "This is my Son, whom I love; with him I am well pleased."

Jesus has been baptized even before he "does" anything; God communicates pleasure with the Son of God. Although Jesus hasn't performed any "ministry" to *please* God, God is nevertheless *pleased with* him. From heaven God proclaims three crucial truths:

- "He's my Son"—an affirmation of the identity of Christ
- "I love him"—an affirmation of the dignity of Jesus and his followers as beloved sons and daughters of God
- "I'm pleased with him"—an affirmation of Jesus' brokenness and poverty of spirit.

Immediately upon this blessing, Jesus is "led by the spirit into the wilderness," where "the tempter" comes to him (Matthew 4:1-11). In Greek, the word for "tempt" is *peirazein*, which more literally means "to test." William Barclay speaks to this as he writes:

> What we call temptation is not meant to make us sin; it is meant to enable us to conquer sin. It is not meant to make us bad, it is meant to make us good. It is not meant to weaken us, it is meant to make us emerge stronger and finer and purer for the ordeal. Temptation is not the penalty of being [human], temptation is the glory of being [human]. It is the test which comes to a [person] whom God wishes to use.[4]

The trademark temptation of Satan (in Greek, *diabolos*, "liar, slanderer") is to become powerful. This encounter is a struggle between power and powerlessness. Satan tempts Jesus at the heart of the very things God proclaimed were true of him.

> The tempter came to him and said, "If you are the Son of God, tell these stones to become bread."
>
> Jesus answered, "It is written: 'People do not live on bread alone, but on every word that comes from the mouth of God.'"

"If you are the Son of God . . ." Satan entices Jesus to make bread out of stones—a temptation to prove his identity by what he does. The desert was lined with little round limestone rocks that must have looked a lot like small loaves of bread. This temptation to use power is a contradiction to the message of powerlessness. The gifts

and strengths God has given us are not for our personal gratification, but for the glory of God's name. We are not simply atomized individuals foraging for whatever power we can scrape together; we're the *beloved sons and daughters of God*.

> Then the devil took him to the holy city and had him stand on the highest point of the temple. "If you are the Son of God," he said, "throw yourself down. For it is written:
> " 'He will command his angels concerning you,
>   and they will lift you up in their hands,
>   so that you will not strike your foot against a stone.'"
> Jesus answered him, "It is also written: 'Do not put the Lord your God to the test.'"

"If you are the Son of God . . ." Satan invites Jesus to throw himself off a building as proof that God loves him enough to keep him safe—a temptation aimed against the belovedness of Jesus. Can God's faithfulness toward the beloved be used for personal gain? Or more to the point—should it?

> Again, the devil took him to a very high mountain and showed him all the kingdoms of the world and their splendor. "All this I will give you," he said, "if you will bow down and worship me."
> Jesus said to him, "Away from me, Satan! For it is written: 'Worship the Lord your God, and serve him only.'"

"Fall down and worship me . . ." Satan promises Jesus power and wealth in exchange for misdirected worship and service—a temptation against the poverty of Jesus' spirit. It's a temptation to compromise, to justify the ends with means that aren't God's plan for our lives. It's a temptation to *have* everything—but Jesus' call was to possess nothing.

It's the same for us. When we listen to the lies that assault our dignity and identity, that manipulate our belovedness, that distract us from God's call to brokenness and poverty of spirit, then we're not living in the fullness of what God desires for us. We must reclaim our broken identity—Jesus' design for our fullness in God.

BROKEN TO HEAL

I first met Nisha when we were visiting her mother in Sonagachi, a district highlighted in the moving documentary *Born into Brothels*. Walking down the two blocks that make up this neighborhood are thousands and thousands of women, most of whom have been trafficked into the commercial sex industry.

I don't think I can ever get used to spending time in red-light districts. There's something about walking into a brothel that stabs deep into my heart. There's something terrible about what a brothel, even an empty one, symbolizes. I doubt that most women working in brothels ever dreamed of growing up having to prostitute themselves. In fact, I doubt that most women working in the commercial sex industry ever had nightmares as bad as the reality of their lives.

Down the main road, then down a small alleyway, Phileena, Courtney Steever (one of the Word Made Flesh staff in the city) and I found the brothel where Nisha's mother worked. Her room was on the second floor. The staircase was dark and narrow, in an old Kolkata building that seemed to be crumbling in on itself.

We knocked on the door. Nisha's mother and another young woman, probably eighteen or nineteen years old, welcomed us into their room and asked that we sit on the bed. I couldn't bring myself to take a seat there. That bed was the symbol of their torment. How many men, maybe twelve or fifteen just the night before and only God knows how many before that, had hurt and abused these young women on that bed? I sat on the floor across from the two women as they ate their lunch of rice and dhal. Beside one of the women sat two-year-old Nisha. Except for the black string tied around her waist, she was naked. She was also bald. Her eyes were beautiful but sad. Her body was frail and tiny, her stomach bloated, indicating the state of her undernourishment.

Courtney and the two women were catching up in Bengali, so I turned my attention to Nisha. I offered her my hand only to be rejected. I was devastated. It suddenly became my goal to get her to play with me. But I knew it wouldn't be easy. In her two-year-old way, she was doing a great job of sassing and hassling me. Pretty humbling having your chops busted by a two-year-old. I kept at it.

I think I understood why she didn't like me. As I sat on the floor of that little room in her brothel, I couldn't help but wonder how many men Nisha had seen use and hurt her mommy. How many men had baby Nisha witnessed climbing onto that bed and taking advantage of her mom? How many had Nisha seen sell her mother as a commodity? Had Nisha ever had any form of healthy affection or appropriate touch from any man?

After maybe fifteen minutes, she finally gave in. It was almost like she had been playing a game with me. This hard-shelled and tough little girl suddenly walked right up to me, and instead of hitting my forehead like she had done several times, she fell into my lap and nestled her head between my shoulder and neck. Suddenly, she just wanted to be held and her smile seemed to stretch all the way across India.

For the next hour, we were friends. Neither of us could really speak to the other, but our smiles and games and touch made a deep impression, at least on me. As I held her tiny body I prayed and prayed for her—pleading with God that her world would be much bigger than the little concrete room with barred windows that she lived in, that her future would be one of hope and fulfilled dreams.

The realist in me feared Nisha would grow up to be groomed into prostitution and very likely pimped out by her mother. Sadly,

Nisha, having been born in a brothel and likely the child of a father she will never be able to trace, could grow up believing that there is no way out. The small room on the second floor of her brothel might be as big as her world ever gets. Like her mother, Nisha may be another innocent, trapped in a horrific cycle, bound by a world that determines her value through her body, even through her soul. What can be done?

The idealist in me (yes, there is an idealist in me, however small) fought back. Looking through the barred window out into the rest of the red-light district, I prayed that the pervading sense of learned helplessness in Sonagachi could be broken by Nisha. I prayed that she would start the revolution in her own neighborhood.

In Word Made Flesh we consider it part of our vocation to be led to God's heart by our friends who are poor. We look to Nisha and are inspired by her potential and her courage as we pray to be transformed. We believe that unless we embrace her and the reality she lives in, the church will have no relevant answers and its good news will lack credibility.

We in the West place people like Nisha in a small box in our overall concept of reality. The truth, however, may be that we are the ones in tiny boxes, insulated and isolated from the very real suffering of people throughout the real world. The reality is that there are some shocking similarities between the learned helplessness in Sonagachi and the learned helplessness of the West. Though we may not recognize it, we live in our own small rooms, unaware of the world beyond or how it can affect us. Could it be that a false sense of self limits our capacity to respond to the opportunities God sets before us? Could values such as security and survival, affection and esteem, and power and control be simply bait that we've gladly taken to? We think these socially and culturally programmed distractions free our minds and open our eyes, but in fact they shut us up in the closets of ignorance and apathy.

TENDING WOUNDS

What would it look like to follow Nisha to God's heart? How could we reimagine a world where Nisha leads and we follow? Is solidarity with her and the millions of victims in the commercial sex industry even a possibility? These questions press me into the mystery of the death and resurrection of Christ.

Joseph, a friend of Jesus, volunteered his tomb to house the dead body of Christ. After the crucifixion

> he took it down, wrapped it in linen cloth and placed it in a tomb cut in the rock, one in which no one had yet been laid. It was Preparation Day, and the Sabbath was about to begin.
>
> The women who had come with Jesus from Galilee followed Joseph and saw the tomb and how his body was laid in it. Then they went home and prepared spices and perfumes. But they rested on the Sabbath in obedience to the commandment.
>
> On the first day of the week, very early in the morning, the women took the spices they had prepared and went to the tomb. They found the stone rolled away from the tomb, but when they entered, they did not find the body of the Lord Jesus. (Luke 23:53–24:3)

I can't imagine how brutal a crucifixion must have been. I can't imagine how thick the nails had to be to hold a squirming and struggling human body to boards or a tree all day long. I can't imagine that once Christ died, the women would have had the upper-body strength to remove those nails themselves. I know I couldn't have done it.

It's terrible to imagine how to remove a dead body from a cross. I can only guess that they would have had to either pull the nails out, aggravating the wounds even more, or pull the body off, leaving the nails embedded in the cross. Either way, the holes in the corpse of Christ, those in his hands or wrists and feet or ankles, must have been gaping, atrocious. I wonder what happened to such gaping holes in the corpse over the course of the forty hours Christ's body was dead.

Because Jesus' death coincided with the commencement of the Sabbath, his corpse was laid in a tomb unattended. The rules regulating activity on the Sabbath prevented the women from immediately dressing what must have been gaping holes in Christ's body. The spices were being prepared by the women to be packed into the open wounds of Jesus' corpse. Upon arriving at the tomb, spices in hand, they were shocked to find his corpse missing.

The symbols here—the Sabbath, the perfumes and spices, the wounds, the corpse of Christ—are important. The Sabbath rest is a contemplative posture. They prepare the perfumes and spices in a state of contemplative stillness and grieving. The women are doing so as a functional deterrent, to tidy up a decayed and rotting corpse. But they are also using materials that are commonly employed as symbols in worship. Spices, perfumes, myrrh, frankincense and other incenses are mentioned throughout Scripture in the context of prayers, offerings and worship. The Bible even tells us that these symbols are present before the throne of God: "golden bowls full of incense, which are the prayers of God's people" (Revelation 5:8).

The women find the tomb empty. Christ has come back to life. But we come to find that his resurrected body still bears those open wounds—those still-fresh lacerations, cuts, gashes and holes.

I have sometimes wondered why, in the great miracle of the resurrection, God didn't heal all the damage done to Christ's physical body? We discover the answer to this when the news gets out that Jesus is back. One of his own disciples, Thomas, has a problem with all this crazy talk. In John 20 he says, "Unless I see the nail marks in his hands and put my finger where the nails were, and put my hand into his side, I will not believe" (verse 25).

Poor Thomas: because of that statement, he'll forever be condemned as "the doubter." Even today, we love to bust his chops. But I'm not *exactly* sure he doubted. All he said was, "Yeah, right. Prove it." A vulgar but maybe accurate parallel example today might be a response to a call from a friend: "Hey man, I was rock climbing with a friend when a guy fell twenty feet and landed on his back! He survived, but his cell phone was in his back pocket and got embedded four inches into the back of his thigh!" My response might be "No way! I don't believe it! And I won't believe it until I stick my hand in his leg and call you from that cell phone."

Sick. But Thomas was right. The wounds were the proof of the crucifixion. And the incident is central to history. Maybe Thomas understood the theological need for Jesus' wounds to be real; maybe he simply wanted his hopes verified. I feel like I can understand.

The fact of Jesus' wounds seemed to be proof to Thomas that Jesus was the Messiah. The echoes of the man who always took bread, blessed it, broke it and gave it now stood before him as the Broken One. The bread now enfleshed in the resurrected body of Christ had to have been broken so that in the miracle of the resurrection it could be given. Thomas's questions, rather than an indication of doubt, might have been an expression of hope for the Broken One on the other side of the cross.

THE BROKEN BODY OF CHRIST

The body is in fact central to this story—both the corpse and the resurrected body of Christ. The metaphor rings throughout Scripture that the worshiping community of Christ is his body (1 Corinthians 12:12-29):

> Just as a body, though one, has many parts, but all its many parts form one body, so it is with Christ. . . .
> God has placed the parts in the body, every one of them,

just as he wanted them to be. If they were all one part, where would the body be? . . .

Those parts of the body that seem to be weaker are indispensable, and the parts that we think are less honorable we treat with special honor. And the parts that are unpresentable are treated with special modesty, while our presentable parts need no special treatment. . . .

If one part suffers, every part suffers with it; if one part is honored, every part rejoices with it.

Now you are the body of Christ, and each one of you is a part of it.

If we are the body of Christ, then where do we find his open wounds today? What do they look like? How can our worship tend to them? Father Emmanuel Katongole, cofounder of the Center for Reconciliation at Duke Divinity School, challenges Christians to find answers to these questions.

> Christian theology and practice needs to point to the power of Christ's cross. In talking about the mystery of the cross, the apostle Paul celebrates Christ's death and resurrection as what has broken down the wall of separation: "you who once were far away have been brought near through the blood of Christ" (Eph 2:13). For Paul, this is the power of Christ's cross: to tear down the wall of separation.[5]

Our prayers, our worship, our praxis of living into a simple spirituality and a grounded theology are all, in a sense, attempts to tend to Christ's open wounds. Unless we have the courage to put our hands into the hurting places of Christ's body—the hurting places of the world—the world won't have reason to trust that God is good.

Nisha, her young mother, and all the women in her neighborhood may well be leading the rest of us to one such wound. If we don't embrace a meaningful humility, community, simplicity, sub-mission and brokenness as part of our faith, such wounds may simply become more and more infected. We can't simply proclaim God's love and sing about it. We need to simply live it.

Not long after our visit to Nisha's home, Phileena and I found ourselves in an old, dilapidated building in the center of Freetown, Sierra Leone. Sitting in a circle with friends, I read this passage from Luke to a group of boys who live on the streets. Many of them, as former child soldiers, have seen (and inflicted) real wounds on real people during a time of civil war.

As I spoke to them of the wounds in Christ's corpse, I asked them to help me figure out what the wounds are in his body today. Quietly, insightfully, profoundly, they touched their own chests and said, "*We* are the open wounds in this body of Christ. We are forgotten, orphaned, homeless."

Thomas got a bad wrap. We bust his chops for doubting, for not having faith. But he was on to something. We must place ourselves in the world and touch our friends who are poor with our lives, touch their wounds—touch Christ's wounds. Thomas's questions still echo today.

Naming these wounds involves a contemplative discovery that ultimately leads to newness in our own vision. Where do we find the imagination to respond? Where do we find the courage to face these wounds? Naming them brings us into a new community of the broken. We befriend those who have been broken by the world we inhabit, and in learning their names we come to learn of our own brokenness. And as Jesus promised his disciples, in the midst of any such broken community, he will be there.

NOW I SEE

Thomas's story ends well. A week after Thomas states he wanted to see and touch the wounds, we find him hanging out with the other disciples behind a locked door. Suddenly Christ is among them. Jesus shows them all his wounds and they believe. Thomas recognizes him and proclaims, "My Lord and my God!"

Thomas, humbled in the presence of his community, is met with a simple presentation from Jesus: "Touch me and see" (Luke 24:39). Thomas's aloof skepticism is broken as he submits to this broken Jesus, whom he proclaims as Lord and God. Thomas's eyes have been opened; he has learned to see.

Sound familiar? Humility. Community. Simplicity. Submission. Brokenness.

With Nisha and those boys in Freetown I felt a bit like Thomas, a bit like that little shepherd David and his sling shot—staring down a big giant. These five small stones—humility, community, simplicity, submission, brokenness—have helped me to see Nisha, Devi, Manolito, Charu, Grace, Bhanu and others. These friends have in turn led me to Christ, and Christ has opened my eyes.

I feel like I've just bent down at a small, dried-up river bank, chose five little rocks, and now need to figure out what to do with them. One of the things I've learned to see, however, is that there's still a lot more I have yet to see. The truth is, there are still some pretty big giants standing in my way of seeing Jesus. But here I stand with five little rocks in my hand. The question will always be: what am I going to do with them? What will *we* do with them?

AFTERWORD

Several years ago I helped start a couple of children's homes in South India. One of the homes was for children who were profoundly disabled, both physically and mentally. One of the first little girls we welcomed into that home was a precious child named Poornima.

Poornima was with us for four-and-a-half years. I remember the day I went to pick her up from the Missionaries of Charity where she had been abandoned. I carried her limp body into the children's home that would become her refuge for the remainder of her short life.

Poornima had no muscle control in her body. She was unable to sit up, let alone feed herself. She was also unable to communicate beyond the cries and moans she would breathe out in moments of need. Poornima was blind and deaf. But after meeting this sweet child, a prominent Chennai businessman remarked, "Through the blind eyes of this child I saw God looking back at me with his love."

Poornima died in the summer of 2000. Each year I visit her gravesite and trust she is in a better place—that her immobilized legs are dancing in paradise, that her blind eyes are opened and drinking in the beauty of our Master, that her deaf ears can now hear God's tender voice affirming eternal and boundless love for our dear sister.

Though she was with us only a short time, she brought joy and love into our home. Poornima will always have a special place in our Word Made Flesh family.

I used to pray for Poornima. I would even sometimes pray that God would give her sight.

As far as my Bible study skills have taken me, it appears that Jesus is the only person in the Scripture to heal someone born blind. I've wondered about that. What's the symbolism in it? Psalm 146:8 tells us clearly that "the Lord gives sight to the blind." In Isaiah 42:1-7 the Scriptures prophesy of the servant of the Lord who will come and "open eyes that are blind." Even Jesus announced his public ministry by reading from the scrolls of Isaiah that he was sent for the "recovery of sight for the blind" (Luke 4:18).

One of the instances when Jesus healed a blind man is a little confusing for me. It seemed like it didn't work. In Mark 8:22-25 Jesus goes to the village of Bethsaida, and a blind man is brought to him. Jesus walks with the blind man outside Bethsaida and then—get ready for this one—spits in the man's blind eyes. He then touches him and asks, "Do you see anything?" The unnamed blind man replies, "I see people; they look like trees walking around."

Wild. Jesus seems to need to do a little more work. So he touches the man's eyes again, and this time the Scripture tells us that the man's eyes "were opened, his sight was restored, and he saw everything clearly." Then Jesus tells him not to even go back to the village.

I don't believe that Jesus messed up on the first try. I think there's something else going on here.

God wants us to see. I wonder if that blind man from the village thought, *Why in the world is this dude spitting on my face!?* And so he resisted the miracle of sight. I think I'm guilty of this more often than not. As I look back on my own faith journey I feel like there are times when I've moved from total blindness to partial sight. Truthfully, as much as I think I want to see, I often limit the vision that

God hopes to give me. My own lack of faith seems to be an obstacle to God's desire to give me everything I need.

But even partial sight can be beautiful. Miracles aside, there really can be a process of growing in vision and growing into sight. I wonder if seeing vague images, people as trees, was necessary to compel that man to have faith for more. I honestly think I still see a lot of people as vague images, like trees. But I too want more.

Pride has humiliated me. Humility has been Christ's spit in my own eyes—an offer and attempt to show me the way to his heart.

Independence still blinds me. The entitled and selfish person inside me resists community. But community has touched my eyes—sometimes even forcing them open to see God and his grace for me.

Affluence and excess tell lies about what I think I want and need. A small and complex virtue, simplicity, gives me a glimpse past the giant things I don't really need so that I can find grace in Christ, my everything.

Oh, the illusion of control and power! Submission allows me to bow my head in order for God to lift my chin and gaze into my eyes. How could we not submit to such a loving and kind God?

Defiance and resistance to a broken God have created the darkest places of blindness. Paradoxically, it's brokenness that is creating wholeness in me.

Funny. I've made things pretty complicated and have been pretty hard on myself. But I'm learning to see that keeping it simple is all it takes to discover God.

EPILOGUE

I found myself sharing about these "Five Stones of Brokenness" for retreats I led in California, Florida and, eventually, Nebraska.

One of those attending the retreat in Nebraska was an art professor at the University of Nebraska-Omaha. Leslie Iwai was inspired by the idea and submitted a sculpture proposal to the Omaha Public Art Commission. The city awarded her a $41,000 grant and made a public park available to display the project.

The project is called *Sounding Stones,* named after hollowed-out stones that are dropped in water to determine its depth. Each stone in the sculpture installation weighs between fourteen and seventeen tons. Inside each hollowed-out center is inscribed the name of one of the five stones of brokenness.[1]

Recently the installation has been moved, but I used to drive by the sculptures on my way to work. I'd see them every day. When I had the courage, I'd look at those fifteen-ton versions of my little stones from the brook of Elah. I'd pray for the ability to accept my limitations and clothe myself not in a self-protective garment of conceit and pride but in the humility of Christ. I'd ask God for the grace to throw myself on the mercies of a community that won't turn a blind eye to my failings but will engage me at my point of need—holding me to a higher standard. I'd pray for the imagination to live into a simplicity that is redemptive and transformational, against the slavery of a consumer society that lies about what I need to have in order to be hip and sassy. I'd plead for a new perspective on submission, one not bracketed by control and success nor jaded by a culture of independence. I'd ask for brokenness, trusting that God dwells among the broken ones of the world, those close to God's heart—like Safi, like the old Muslim man from the House for the Dying, like Grace, like Manolito, like Nisha, like those I count as friends and family from the red-light districts, refugee camps and slums of the world.

My friends. My guides. My sounding stones. Those who help me to see. My eyes.

ACKNOWLEDGMENTS

Simple Spirituality is the first "feature-length" writing project I've ever worked on. I've written and published a number of chapters for other books and my fair share of articles, but writing a whole book was a bigger endeavor than I could have prepared myself for.

Unraveling the thoughts in my head regarding spirituality was no easy feat. Wrapping language around them was even harder. For the assistance I was generously given in this process, I am deeply grateful. I ask in advance for the forgiveness of anyone I fail to mention here. There have been so many friends who have journeyed with me on this process, and sadly there's not room to mention all of you by name.

Phileena, you have always been the best friend I could have ever dreamed of or hoped for. Thank you for believing in me and my voice. Thank you for affirming my vision for this book and standing with me in it. Thank you for making creative space for me to tap away on a laptop keyboard late at night and early in the morning and throughout our sabbatical. Your love for me fueled my work and has been an inspiration.

There were many people who found the courage to peek at early drafts of this manuscript. Among the bravest and most innovative with their suggestions were Amey Victoria Adkins, Thomas (you'll always be "Brent" to me) Graeve, Bethel Lee, Mandy Mowers,

Rachelle Serlet and Emily Timm. Thank you for not reminding me that I should have learned grammar and spelling in primary school. Your technical assistance and gentle nudges toward better content have gone a long, long way. Thank you for seeing possibilities in the primordial stages of what this book was and helping to grow it up a bit more. Your fingerprints are all over this in so many ways and it's a much better piece because of each of you.

In a world short on role models, my editor David Zimmerman is a real live super hero. No joke, I've seen video of him in a cape and tights. For real. David, you have been an incredible friend and companion on this journey. Thanks for your thoughtfulness as you guided the content. Thanks for demystifying the writing and publishing process. Thanks for keeping it clean and cutting out all the cuss words I tried to sneak past you. Props to you for negotiating with the "diva" in me—I'm still holding out for author-inspired bobble-heads, action figures and cell-phone charms. Thanks for helping me not look like an idiot (more or less). I have been so honored to have worked with you and will miss the time and space for what has been some really fun collaboration.

The final stages of writing this book happened while Phileena and I were on sabbatical at the Center for Reconciliation at Duke Divinity School. We are both deeply grateful for the envelope of peace and rest Duke offered us. So much love and thanks goes out to Father Emmanuel Katongole, Chris Rice and those of you who warmly welcomed and embraced us while we were with you. Thank you for giving me the time and space to finish this project and for all the encouragement and excitement about it.

Of course, I want to thank the entire Word Made Flesh community for supporting me in the writing of this book. That I write about our shared spirituality is really a reflection of our collective vocational yearnings for more. Thank you for being Christ in the world. Thank you for your courage in following our friends who are poor to God's heart. Thank you for every single sacrifice you've made to love Christ in the parts of the world where his heart breaks today.

Specifically, I want to thank our board of directors for believing in the value of writing and encouraging me to take time to work on this. I also want to thank our Omaha community for giving me a few extra hours to steal away from the office to work on this. I pray that this book gives voice to our friends and finds its way to people who would hold us up in prayer as we continue to fight for justice, equality and the affirmation of human dignity.

Since 1993 I have needed the faithful prayers and support of friends and family to be part of the community in which I serve. It goes without saying, but I'm gonna say it anyway, that without each of you standing with Phileena and me we could never have gotten this far. I pray that everything you've sacrificed for us would be returned to you in simple and beautiful ways. Thank you for your faithfulness. Thank you for your generosity. Thank you for your love. Your kindness to us has meant so very much and has gone such a long, long way.

Finally, my prayer is that in every way, I can be an authentic friend to my brothers and sisters who suffer. In no way do I believe there are "voiceless" people, rather people whose voices we have turned down, muted and ignored. You, my dear ones, are champions of this world. It's your voices that we must hear. Thank you for pointing us to Christ. Thank you for leading us to God's heart. Thank you for opening your lives to me and allowing yourself to be the prophetic presence of Jesus in my life. Countless faces and names rush to mind, but I acknowledge a few: Tuna, Samulee, Tinku, Sudeep, Suryakala, Yasotha, Sindujah, Divya, Sheela, Shembu, Narayani, Arun, Prema, Safi, Ana Mania, Bhavani, Rupa, Dipa, Priya, Christine, Martin, Veronica, Charo, Ruth and Betsy, Carlos, Tatiana, Lydia, Kati, Vali, Moises, Anna, June, Marie, Veronica and Victoria, Emilia, the Fazluis, the Syeds and Prabha's family—you and so many others have saved me. Thank you for your love. Thank you for fighting for more. Thank you for believing in a good God when everything around you causes you to doubt.

To each of you who picked this book up, thank you for opening your heart and mind to this journey.

Take it slow, keep it simple, and bless God.

NOTES

Introduction: On Sight, Spirituality and Stones

[1]I have intentionally sought to refer to a trinitarian concept of God that celebrates God the Father, Jesus Christ the Son, and the Holy Spirit. When referring to God I have tried to avoid pronouns loaded with gender assumptions or forms.

[2]In Word Made Flesh we have sought to reclaim the distance created by referring to our friends as "the poor." Though much of the world is in fact very poor, many of them are theologically our brothers and sisters, all of them our neighbors. Our community collectively embraces a vocation that seeks to identify with the poverty of our friends as an effort and attempt to humanize all of humanity.

[3]In writing about my "blindness," I do not wish to take anything away from those who literally cannot see. I was sensitized as a child to this because my adopted younger brother was legally blind. Today my spiritual director, who is physically blind, seems to see right through me every time I visit him. He's perhaps the most perceptive person I have met in my entire life.

[4]Dr. Kinlaw once told me over tea, "Chris, I don't have time for good books, only the best."

[5]José Saramago, Blindness (New York: Harvest, 1997), p. 324.

[6]Father Larry Gillick, S.J., "Food for Thought," St. John's Parish Newsletter, Creighton University, Omaha, Nebraska, October 29, 2006, p. 4.

[7]Thomas Keating, The Human Condition: Contemplation and Transformation (New York: Paulist Press, 1999), pp. 13, 9.

[8]For more on the conference, see The United States of America Department of State in collaboration with the War Against Trafficking Alliance (Shared Hope International, International Justice Mission, Johns Hopkins University/Protection Project and the Salvation Army), Pathbreaking

Strategies in the Global Fight Against Sex Trafficking—Prevention, Protection, Prosecution: Conference Recommendations (Washington, D.C., February 23-26, 2003).

[9]This wasn't uncommon in antiquity. In a society where the individual submitted his or her identity to the collective personality, a duel between champions would often decide the fate of all. William Sanford LaSor, David Allan Hubbard and Frederic Wm. Bush, *Old Testament Survey: The Message, Form, and Background of the Old Testament* (Grand Rapids: Eerdmans, 1982), p. 239.

[10]It gets a little messy at this point: David takes Goliath's sword and cuts the head off of his corpse. I'm sure an awful, bloody mess. Not for kids—at least this part of the story.

[11]Quoted from Bono's speech at the National Prayer Breakfast, Washington, D.C., February 2, 2006.

[12]Vincenzo Sardi, "Goliath Was Shot with a .38!," *Weekly World News*, October 23, 2001, pp. 14-15.

[13]Of course, this is disputed as well as convoluted. Some accounts state that Goliath only had two or three brothers, while other accounts suggest Goliath was actually from an entire tribe of giants. Among various sources, see Louis Ginzberg, *The Legends of the Jews: Bible Times and Characters from Joshua to Esther*, trans. Henrietta Szold Radin (Philadelphia: Jewish Publication Society of America, 1913), p. 31; Howard Jacobson, *A Commentary on Pseudo-Philo's Liber Antiquitatum Biblicarum: With Latin Text and English Translation* (New York: Brill Academic, 1996), 2:1184; W. M. Thomson, D.D., *The Land and the Book, or, Biblical Illustrations Drawn from the Manners and Customs, the Scenes and Scenery of the Holy Land* (Franklin Square, N.Y.: Harper & Brothers, 1859), p. 360; and Sir Edward Thomason's *Memoirs During Half a Century* (London: Longman, Brown, and Longmans, 1845), 2:58.

Chapter 1: Humility

[1]Francois de Salignac de La Mothe Fenelon, *Christian Perfection* (Minneapolis: Bethany Fellowship, 1975), p. 205.

[2]Klaus Wengst, *Humility: Solidarity of the Humiliated* (London: SCM Press, 1988), p. 49.

[3]Wayne A. Mack with Joshua Mack, *Humility: The Forgotten Virtue* (Phillipsburg, N.J.: P & R Publishing, 2005), pp. 21-23. The authors suggest much more than my simplistic rendering of their thesis. However, the book stings of formulaic solutions that perpetuate the myth of virtue without a connection point to a sincere relationship with God. The book does end

up exploring the dynamics of God's character, but the authors tendency is to replace devotion with duty, a subtle yet profound difference.

[4]J. B. Phillips, *Your God Is Too Small* (New York: Collier/Macmillan, 1961).

[5]Sadly and to our surprise, the bulls were actually killed—six that very afternoon—and so, to the dismay of many sitting around us, Phileena and I gregariously cheered for the bulls (although not against the matadors).

[6]Desmond Tutu, *God Has a Dream: A Vision of Hope for Our Times* (New York: Image Books/Doubleday, 2004), p. 82.

[7]Fenelon, *Christian Perfection,* p. 207.

Chapter 2: Community

[1]Dietrich Bonhoeffer, *Life Together: A Discussion of Christian Fellowship* (San Francisco: HarperSanFrancisco, 1954), p. 112.

[2]I have tried to repress some of my pee-wee league memories because I vaguely remember striking out while playing tee-ball—hard to believe, but yes, it's true.

[3]What I mean by "sins of tribalism" was, for the good of all, tastefully removed from this book by my editor. But for the record, I am a Nebraska football fan, and the serious college football fan out of a sense of tribalism can hardly affirm the human dignity of the fans of several other teams (you know who you are). In all seriousness, the industry of college and professional sports is an indictment of the real problems related to affirming and fighting for human dignity. In his book *No Salvation Outside the Poor* (Maryknoll, N.Y.: Orbis, 2008), Father Jon Sobrino writes, "The three best soccer players in the world—an Englishman, a Frenchman, and a Brazilian, who all play on the same Spanish team—earn U.S. $42 million a year; by comparison the San Salvador (El Salvador's capital) metropolitan area, with 1,821,532 inhabitants, has an annual budget of $45.6 million. This is comparative harm, a shameless insult to the poor, a failure of the human family. In theological language it is the failure of God in creation" (pp. 25-26).

[4]Chris Sugden, *Seeking the Asian Face of Jesus: The Practice and Theology of Christian Social Witness in Indonesia and India 1974-1996* (Oxford: Regnum, 1997), p. 183.

[5]Ibid.

[6]John Stott, *The Lausanne Covenant: An Exposition and Commentary* (Minneapolis: World Wide Publications, 1975), p. 27.

[7]Leonardo Boff and Clovis Boff, *Introducing Liberation Theology* (Maryknoll, N.Y.: Orbis, 1998), p. 31.

[8]Sugden, *Seeking the Asian Face of Jesus,* pp. 183-209.

[9]These reflections on Nouwen's three lies come from a series of messages

he gave during appearances on Crystal Cathedral Ministries' *Hour of Power* television show in 1992.

[10]Jon Sobrino, *The Principle of Mercy: Taking the Crucified People from the Cross* (Maryknoll, N.Y.: Orbis, 1994), p. 7.

[11]Ibid., pp. 29-30. Our community has adopted the language "Majority World" to replace terms such as the Third World, Two-Thirds World, the Fourth World (the poorest of the "Third World" nations), Developing Countries, the Underdeveloped World, the South, the Global South, Less Economically Developed Countries (LEDC), and Least Developed Countries. "Majority World" is an accurate representation of the fact that most of the world's population are, in fact, poor.

[12]Jürgen Moltmann, *The Crucified God: The Cross of Christ as the Foundation and Criticism of Christian Theology* (Minneapolis: Fortress Press, 1993), p. 51.

[13]Jean Vanier, *The Broken Body: Journey to Wholeness* (London: Darton, Longman and Todd, 1988), p. 1.

[14]Father Sobrino shared these things during a meeting the Word Made Flesh Field Directors had with him in San Salvador, El Salvador, on January 15, 2003.

[15]Though I'm sure these ideas have been formally recorded by Jayakumar somewhere, he often brings these questions up in his teaching and speaking.

[16]I have often written about these friends and neighbors and have shared versions of this story in the following publications: "Discovering the Poor Outside Majestic Colony" in *Good News Magazine*, March/April 1998, pp. 12-19; "Discovering Holiness in Ministry Among the Poor," in *Power, Holiness, and Evangelism*, ed. Randy Clark (Shippensburg, Penn.: Destiny Image, 1999), pp. 74-85; "Outside the Majestic Colony," in *Lifeline: Sharing Christ in a Broken World*, ed. Steve Beard and Maggie Schroeder (Wilmore, Ky.: Living Streams, 2003), pp. 107-27.

[17]David Chronic, "Towards Community," *The Cry: The Advocacy Journal of Word Made Flesh* 6, no. 2 (summer 2000), p. 15.

[18]Mother Teresa, *No Greater Love* (Novato, Calif.: New World Library, 1997), pp. 40-41.

[19]Frances O'Gorman, *Charity and Change: From Bandaid to Beacon* (Victoria: World Vision Australia, 1992), p. 67.

[20]Jayakumar Christian, in e-mail correspondence.

[21]Viv Grigg, *Companion to the Poor: Christ in the Urban Slums* (Monrovia, Calif.: MARC Publications, 1990), p. 80.

[22]Henri J. M. Nouwen, Donald P. MacNeill and Douglas A. Morrison, *Com-*

passion: A Reflection of the Christian Life (New York: Image, 1982), p. 57. Italics in the original.

[23] Jean Vanier, *Becoming Human* (New York: Paulist Press, 1998), p. 60.

[24] Kim Comer, comp. and ed., *Wisdom of the Sadhu: Teachings of Sundar Singh* (Maryknoll, N.Y.: Plough, 2000), pp. 134-37.

[25] Ibid., p. 136.

Chapter 3: Simplicity

[1] Rick Vecchio, "Script for a Triumph Turns into Peruvian President's Dark Day," AP Wire Report (July 29, 2000).

[2] Read my blog post about my misadventures in Tamil at <http://ifiblogged.tumblr.com/post/27113120>.

[3] Joel B. Green, *The Theology of the Gospel of Luke* (Cambridge: Cambridge University Press, 1995), p. 113.

[4] Christine Pohl, *Making Room: Recovering Hospitality as a Christian Tradition* (Grand Rapids: Eerdmans, 1999), p. 30.

[5] Sandra Wheeler, *Wealth as Peril and Obligation: The New Testament on Possession* (Grand Rapids: Eerdmans, 1995), p. 83.

[6] Pohl, Making Room, p. 12.

[7] Wheeler, *Wealth as Peril and Obligation*, p. 72.

[8] Khalil Gibran, *The Prophet* (New York: Phoenix Press/Walter & Company, 1986), p. 37.

[9] A version of this story can also be found in "Living and Responding to Heal and Transform," in *Sexually Exploited Children: Working to Protect and Heal*, ed. Phyllis Kilbourn and Marjorie McDermid (Monrovia, Calif.: MARC Publications, 1998), pp. 83-91.

[10] E. Stanley Jones, *The Unshakable Kingdom and the Unchanging Person* (Bellingham, Wash.: McNett Press, 1995), p. 153.

[11] Charles Edward White, "What Wesley Practiced and Preached About Money," *Leadership* 8, no. 1 (winter 1987): 27-29.

[12] Richard J. Foster, *Freedom of Simplicity* (New York: HarperCollins, 1981), p. 147.

[13] Douglas Coupland, *JPod* (New York: Bloomsbury, 2006), p. 7.

[14] David E. Shi, *The Simple Life: Plain Living and High Thinking in American Culture* (New York: Oxford University Press, 1985), p. 280.

[15] Foster, *Freedom of Simplicity*, p. 141.

[16] David Chronic, "Beyond Simplicity," *The Cry: The Advocacy Journal of Word Made Flesh* 7, no. 1 (spring 2001): 6.

[17] Raniero Cantalamessa, *Poverty* (New York: Alba House, 1997), p. 23.

[18] Omer Englebert, *St. Francis of Assis: A Biography* (Ann Arbor, Mich.: Servant, 1979), p. 72.

[19]Cantalamessa, *Poverty*, p. 47.

[20]Chronic, "Beyond Simplicity," p. 14.

Chapter 4: Submission

[1]Henri J. M. Nouwen, *Intimacy* (San Francisco: HarperSanFrancisco, 1969), p. 31.

[2]M. E. P. Seligman, S. F. Maler and J. Geer, "The alleviation of learned helplessness in the dog," *Journal of Abnormal Psychology* 78 (1968): 256-62, as cited in *Street Children: A Guide to Effective Ministry*, ed. Phyllis Kilborn (Monrovia, Calif.: MARC Publications, 1997), p. 160.

[3]United Nations, "State of the World's Women," Voluntary Fund for the UN Decade for Women, New York, 1979.

[4]Ibid., pp. 60-61.

[5]Sue Monk Kidd, *Dance of the Dissident Daughter: A Woman's Journey from Christian Tradition to the Sacred Feminine* (San Francisco: HarperSanFrancisco, 1995), p. 21.

[6]See *Adbusters* 10, no 1 (January/February 2002): 30-31, for a shocking juxtaposition of an Afghani woman covered from head to toe in a burka across from a photo of a Western, white, blond, thin woman coming out of plastic surgery with a bloody, bandaged nose.

[7]Desmond Tutu, *God Has a Dream: A Vision of Hope for Our Time* (New York: Image/Doubleday, 2004), p. 48.

[8]For an accessible and fresh reflection on Paul's discussion of submission in Ephesians, see Rob Bell's book *Sex God: Exploring the Endless Connections Between Sexuality and Spirituality* (Grand Rapids: Zondervan, 2007), pp. 111-27. Verse 21, though usually disconnected from the rest of the chapter (one of the great travesties of biblical hermeneutics), is the preamble to Paul's teaching on submission in marriage. Sadly, verse 22 has been given much attention out of context to justify a repressive dominance of husbands over their wives. Actually, the English translation inserts the word submit while in the Greek it is merely implied. Typically, this passage has been misused to demand submission from Christian wives while absolving the burden of submission as love from the husband.

[9]C. S. Lewis, *The Four Loves* (San Diego: Harcourt Brace, 1988), pp. 105-6, emphasis added.

[10]Francis Bacon, *Of Empire* (New York: Penguin Books, 2005), p. 17.

[11]Jayakumar Christian, *God of the Empty-Handed: Poverty, Power, and the Kingdom of God* (Monrovia, Calif.: MARC Publications, 1999), p. 6.

[12]Ibid., p. 7.

[13]Ibid., p. 8.

[14]Ibid.

[15]W. Heywood, trans., "Ugolino di Monte Santa Maria," in *The Little Flowers of St. Francis of Assisi* (New York: Vintage Spiritual Classics, 1998), p. 9.

[16]See Samuel T. Kamaleson, "Mangoes and Marbles," *Decision*, January 1978, and *Insight*, fall 1979.

[17]Bob Marley, *Talk'n Blues,* Polygram Records, February 5, 1991.

Chapter 5: Brokenness

[1]C.S. Lewis, *The Great Divorce* (New York: Collier, 1946), pp. 98-105.

[2]Ibid., pp. 104-5.

[3]Henri Nouwen, "Moving from Solitude to Community to Ministry," *Leadership* (spring 1995): 84.

[4]William Barclay, *The Gospel of Matthew,* 2 vols. (Philadelphia: Westminster Press, 1975), 1:63.

[5]From an unpublished paper by Emmanuel Katongole, "AIDS, Africa and the 'Age of Miraculous Medicine': Naming the Silences" or "Recovering an African Theological Voice in the Wake of AIDS and in the Age of Miraculous Medicine," Catholic Theological Ethics in the World Church, an international conference for Catholic theological ethicists, Padua, Italy, July 8-11, 2006. The paper will be published in *Applied Ethics in a World Church*, ed. Linda Hogan (Maryknoll, N.Y.: Orbis, 2008).

Epilogue

[1]See Joseph Morton, "'Stones' Meaning Depends on Who Is Doing the Viewing," *Omaha World Herald,* November 19, 2004, pp. 1-2.

LIKEWISE. *Go and do.*

A man comes across an ancient enemy, beaten and left for dead. He lifts the wounded man onto the back of a donkey and takes him to an inn to tend to the man's recovery. Jesus tells this story and instructs those who are listening to "go and do likewise."

Likewise books explore a compassionate, active faith lived out in real time. When we're skeptical about the status quo, Likewise books challenge us to create culture responsibly. When we're confused about who we are and what we're supposed to be doing, Likewise books help us listen for God's voice. When we're discouraged by the troubled world we've inherited, Likewise books encourage us to hold onto hope.

In this life we will face challenges that demand our response. Likewise books face those challenges with us so we can act on faith.

likewisebooks.com